P9-CQH-017

ENDANGERED PLANET

Previous page: A logger saws through a rain forest tree trunk in Cameroon, central Africa.

▼ Built in a former quarry in Cornwall, England, the Eden Project is home to more than 5,000 types of plants from all the different climatic zones of the world. Plants are vital for life on Earth because they collect the Sun's energy and release the oxygen that we breathe. The Eden Project attempts to get across an important message: we need plants, but at the same time we are making it hard for many of them to survive.

KFK KINGFISHER KNOWLEDGE

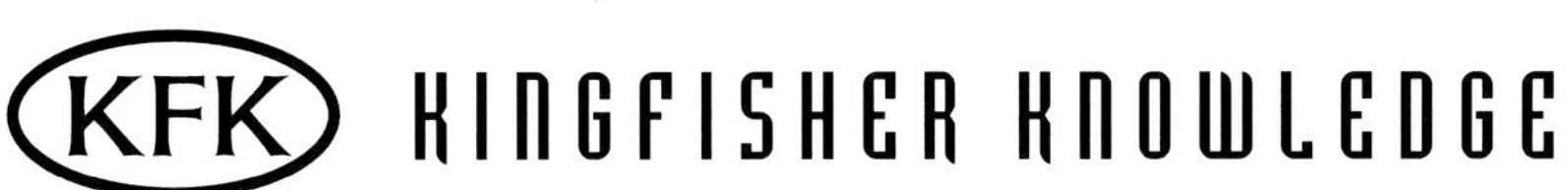

ENDANGERED PLANET

David Burnie

Foreword by
Tony Juniper

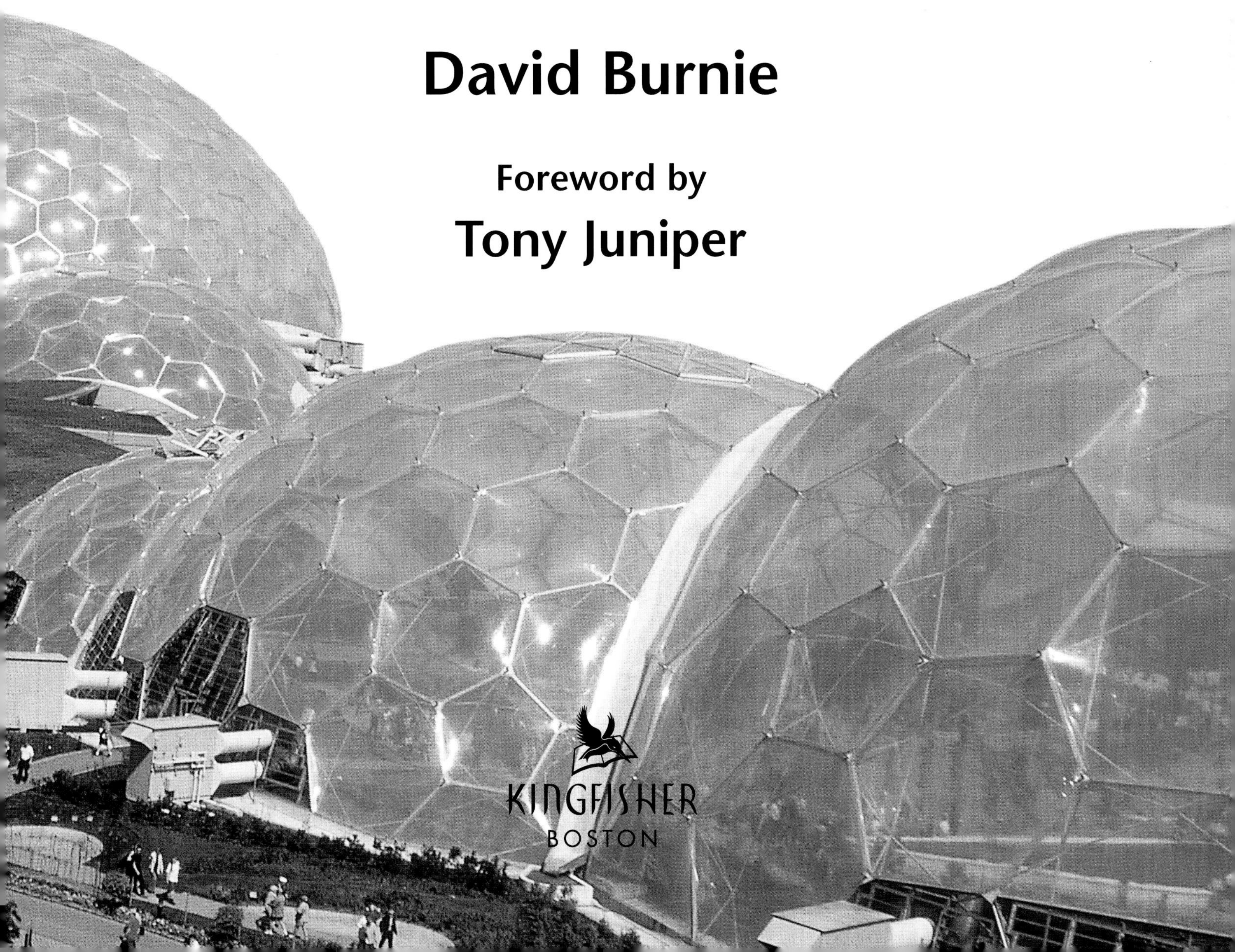

KINGFISHER
BOSTON

Managing editor: Russell Mclean
Coordinating editor: Stephanie Pliakas
Senior designer: Peter Clayman
Picture researcher: Kate Miller
Production controller: Lindsey Scott
DTP manager: Nicky Studdart
DTP operator: Primrose Burton
Artwork archivists: Wendy Allison, Jenny Lord
Proofreaders: Jennifer Schofield,
Sarah Snavely
Indexer: Sue Lightfoot

KINGFISHER
a Houghton Mifflin Company imprint
222 Berkeley Street
Boston, Massachusetts 02116
www.houghtonmifflinbooks.com

First published in 2004
10 9 8 7 6 5 4 3 2
1SBF/1107/TWP/MA(MA)/130ENSOMA/F

LIBRARY OF CONGRESS CATALOGING-IN-PUBLICATION DATA
Burnie, David.
Endangered planet/David Burnie.—1st ed.
p. cm.—(Kingfisher knowledge)
Includes index.
1. Nature—Effect of human beings on. 2. Environmental degradation. 3.Environmental pollution. 4. Environmental responsibility. I. Title. II.Series.
GF75.B87 2004
333.95—dc22
2004000478

ISBN 978-0-7534-5776-4

Printed in Singapore

GO FURTHER . . .
INFORMATION PANEL KEY:

web sites and further reading

career paths

places to visit

Contents

NOTE TO READERS

The web site addresses listed in this book are correct at the time of going to print. However, due to the ever-changing nature of the Internet, web site addresses and content can change. Web sites can contain links that are unsuitable for children. The publisher cannot be held responsible for changes in web site addresses or content or for information obtained through third-party web sites. We strongly advise that Internet searches should be supervised by an adult.

▼ Pools of oil surround drilling rigs in Azerbaijan on the edge of the Caspian Sea. This central Asian country contains some of the most polluted shores in the world.

Chapter 2
Planet under pressure 19

Chapter 3
Sustainable world 45

Foreword

Never before in the long history of Earth has one species—humankind—had such a dramatic impact on the planet that sustains all known life. Recent decades in particular have seen a rapid acceleration in the rate of environmental change. Today people are altering the world's climate and using up more resources than ever before. We are even on the verge of causing the extinction of more species than at any time since the dinosaurs disappeared around 66 million years ago.

Each year the world's growing population demands more food, energy, household products, freshwater, places to live, cars, and roads. All of these things cause some impact on the world around us. Forests and wetlands are cleared to make space for farms, mines are dug out to reach minerals, harmful pollution is released from different industries, while the use of energy in our houses, cars, and factories is causing changes to the climate.

My environmental work has taken me to many different countries, and in each place the challenges are different. In very poor countries people need to find ways to provide food, water, and housing while still preserving their amazing rain forests and other wildlife habitats. In rich countries the environment could be better protected by cutting pollution, saving energy, and using fewer resources—by recycling more, for example. In the end, however, every single one of us relies on the same Earth, so all of us need to help take care of it—no matter where we live.

When I was a child and first became aware of threats to the environment, few people knew about pollution or disappearing wildlife. Today things are different. More and more people know that they must work harder to protect our world, and they are making changes to do just that. Where I live, in England, some types of pollution have been cleaned up or reduced, and some wild animals are coming back after almost disappearing forever.

Saving the environment is really about common sense: making sure the best places for wildlife are taken care of, reducing waste, using cars less often, saving energy, and using the best new technologies to minimize pollution. But most important of all, it is about caring for people—especially the world's poorest people. Giving everyone in the world a good life, while preserving all of the wildlife, stopping pollution, and not changing the climate, is a huge challenge. But it can be done.

During the many years that I have worked to save the environment I have seen a lot of different solutions and have met many people who know how to solve environmental problems. But saving the environment is not only for experts. Everyone needs to play a part because all of the big environmental issues are caused and solved by the little things done by you and me. So read this fascinating book, and learn something about the big questions that are facing every one of us who lives on this small planet. Above all, don't be worried, but do think about how you can do your part to help. It's a beautiful world—let's take care of it.

Tony Juniper

Tony Juniper, Executive Director, Friends of the Earth
www.foei.org

Ring-tailed lemur, Madagascar

CHAPTER 1

Fragile Earth

By the time you read this book, life may have been found on another planet—the most likely place being Mars. The chances are low, but if this happens, it will be a very important event because it will mean that Earth is not alone. From all we know about the universe, Earthlike planets are rare. If space exploration does uncover alien life, it is likely to be simple and microscopic, like the bacteria on Earth today. Our planet has sustained life for almost four billion years, and during that time millions of different species have developed. Life has adapted to all types of changes, from ice ages to catastrophic meteorite strikes. But after this long and varied past something remarkable has happened: a species has evolved that dominates Earth. That species is us, and the planet's future is in our hands.

The living planet

Life on Earth probably began by accident through a chain of chemical reactions over a very long period of time. But why did life begin here and not on any other planet? One reason is that Earth is just the right distance from the Sun. It gets enough heat to keep it warm but not so much that it boils. Earth also has an atmosphere, which protects the surface from harmful rays. Finally, it is covered by water—a perfect substance for the development of living things.

▲ Earth's atmosphere is like a protective coat that shields living things. The northern lights—seen here over Alaska—are caused by high-energy particles from the Sun that plunge into our atmosphere.

▶ This diagram shows the thinness of the biosphere compared to the planet as a whole. The biosphere is like a living skin, stretched over the entire surface of Earth.

The biosphere

Although Earth is home to life, more than 99.999 percent of the planet is strictly off-limits to living things. The outer atmosphere is much too cold, while most of Earth's crust is much too hot. Sandwiched in between is the biosphere—a zone where living things can survive. Compared to the entire planet, the biosphere is extremely thin. At its deepest, it measures only 15.5 mi. (25km) from top to bottom or around 45 times the height of the tallest structure ever built. This wraparound layer is our home, and it is one that we share with every other form of life on Earth. Inside the biosphere matter and energy are always on the move. Vital substances, such as water and carbon, travel between living things and their surroundings, while energy pours into the biosphere from the Sun. All around planet Earth the whole biosphere bustles with growth and activity.

Energy and living things

Energy is the driving force that keeps living things working. Our energy comes from food, but the things that we eat also have to obtain energy. If you trace your way back through this chain of energy, you end up with plants. Instead of getting energy from other living things, plants make it for themselves through a process called photosynthesis, which takes place inside their leaves. Through photosynthesis plants trap the energy in sunlight and use it to build substances that they need in order to grow. This remarkable trick is also performed by microscopic algae, which drift in billions throughout the seas. Because photosynthesis creates food, it powers almost all life on Earth. If it stopped tomorrow, every living thing—except for a few specialized bacteria—would slowly but surely die out.

Is there life anywhere else?

Despite years of listening, looking, and waiting, scientists haven't detected any signs of life beyond our own solar system. Many experts think that it exists, but with such vast distances separating us from other stars, their hunch cannot be proved. Within the solar system the task is much easier because space probes can visit other planets and search there for signs of life. So far this exploration has revealed some tantalizing hints of past life on Mars but no definite proof. Farther away, some of the moons of Jupiter and Saturn seem to contain liquid water, which would make it possible that life could have started there. The hunt continues, but so far we have no positive results—our planet seems to be unique.

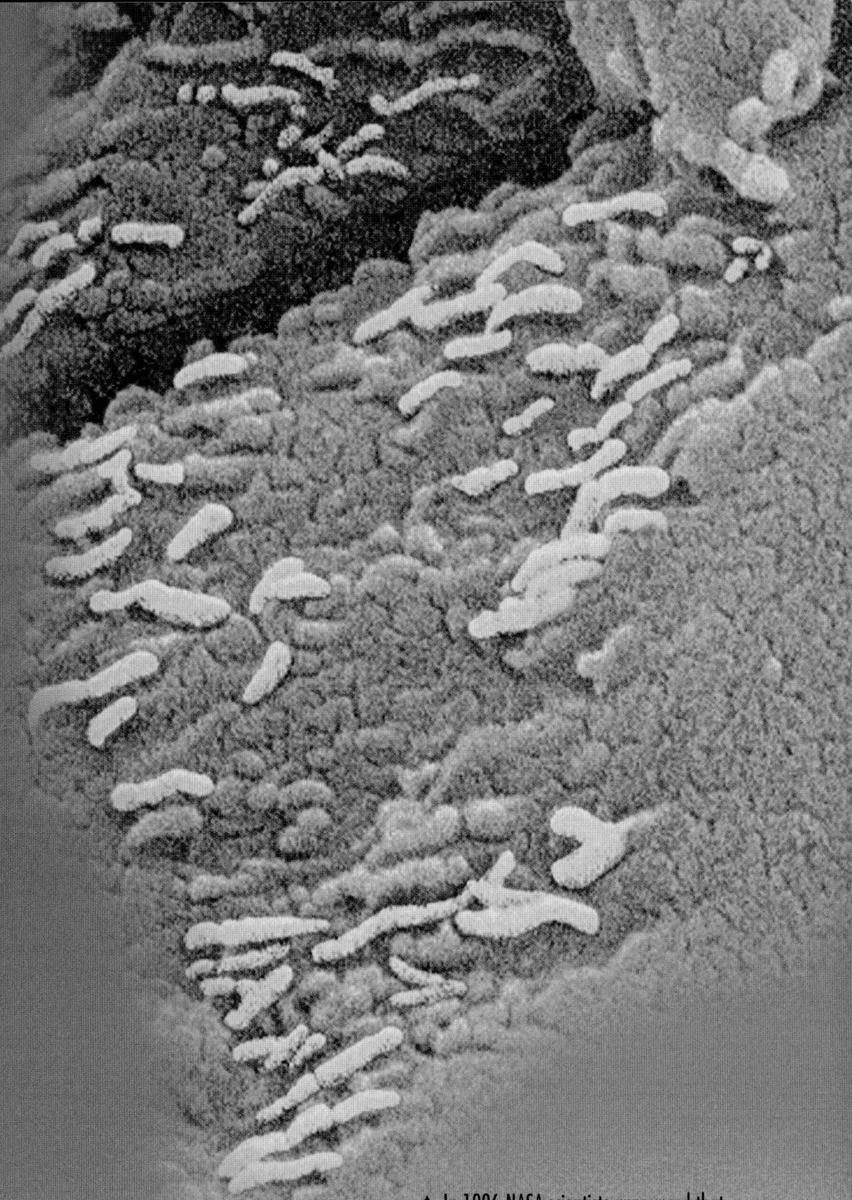

▲ In 1996 NASA scientists announced that the yellow objects on this Martian meteorite could be the fossils of ancient bacteria. Since then most experts have changed their minds. In spite of this reassessment, Mars still looks like the most promising place for life beyond Earth.

◀ As the Sun sets over Africa's grasslands, plants and animals put its energy to work. Plants collect only around one percent of the solar energy that falls on Earth, but this is enough to power almost every living thing on the planet. The only exceptions are certain bacteria that get energy from minerals in Earth's crust.

Natural cycles

When a river plunges over a waterfall, it is playing a part in an endless cycle that keeps all the world's water moving. Although we cannot see it happening, many other essential substances, such as carbon and nitrogen, move in cycles too. These natural cycles are vital for living things because they deliver life's chemical ingredients and remove them after they have been used.

▲ At Niagara Falls, between Canada and the U.S., water plunges almost 200 ft. (60m) on its journey toward the sea. Freshwater makes up less than one percent of all the liquid water in the world.

The water cycle

Every day the Sun's energy evaporates around one trillion tons of water out of the world's seas. This incredible lifting operation marks the start of the hydrological cycle, or water cycle. From there, things literally go downhill. The water vapor condenses into clouds that produce rain or snow. Sooner or later this moisture makes its way back to the sea. The water cycle is crucial to all life, but it is especially important on land. On land rainfall helps shape the world's living communities, or biomes (see page 15). The water cycle also shapes the surface of Earth because rain slowly erodes even the hardest rocks, creating valleys and floodplains as it sweeps sediment toward the sea.

▲ During a forest fire the carbon stored in living trees is suddenly combined with oxygen and released back into the air as carbon dioxide. Plants also release their carbon when they die since microbes—tiny living things such as bacteria—gradually break them down.

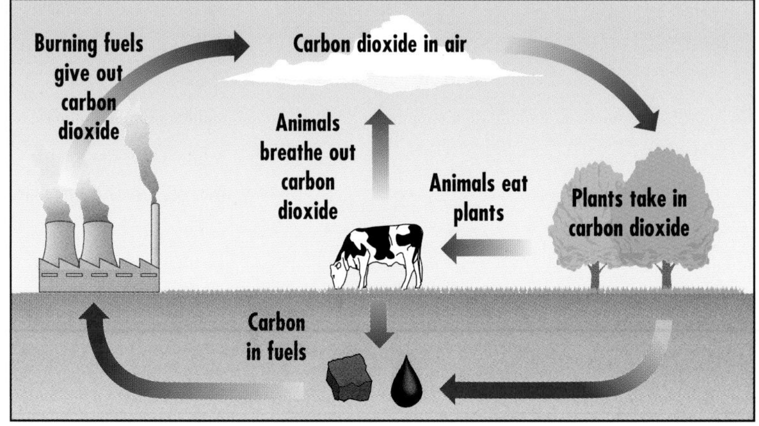

▲ This simplified version of the carbon cycle shows how carbon dioxide travels between the air and living things. In other parts of the cycle carbon dioxide is absorbed and released by the sea. Some of this carbon becomes built in to seabed sediment, which is then transformed into rocks.

The carbon cycle

Life is based on carbon, a chemical element that is amazingly good at forming different compounds (mixtures of two or more chemical ingredients). On Earth pure carbon is rare. Instead the carbon cycle centers around carbon dioxide, a gas that makes up around 0.03 percent of the atmosphere. With the help of energy from sunlight, plants collect this gas, and they use it to build complex carbon compounds that they need in order to grow. When animals eat plants—or each other—the reverse happens: carbon compounds are broken down, and their energy and carbon dioxide are released. This part of the cycle is fast, but carbon sometimes becomes trapped for millions of years. This happens when dead remains become buried and slowly turn into coal or oil. If these fuels are dug up and burned, ancient carbon suddenly floods back into the air.

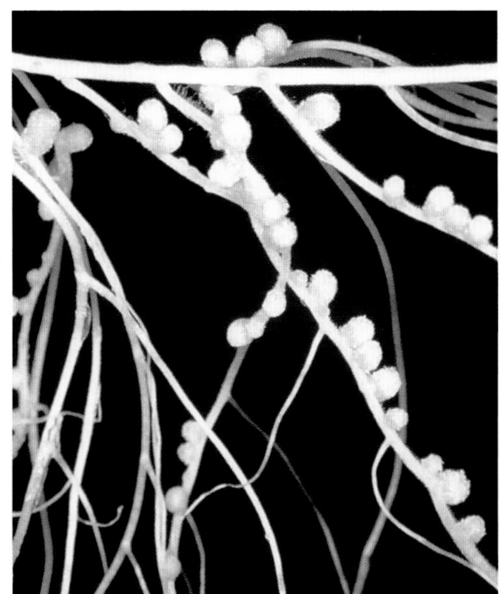

◀ Like beads on a necklace, nodules sprout from the roots of a pea plant. Each nodule contains millions of nitrogen-fixing bacteria that help the plant grow. The plant forms the nodules in order to encourage bacteria to move in.

▲ Lightning "fixes" nitrogen when it flashes through the sky. Later, when it rains, this fixed nitrogen is washed into the soil. Nitrogen is also fixed by cars, which pump it out of their exhausts.

The nitrogen cycle

Unlike carbon dioxide, nitrogen is extremely plentiful, making up 78 percent of the atmosphere. All living things need it, but strangely, very few can use pure nitrogen from the air. Instead plants collect nitrogen that has been "fixed," or chemically converted, by bacteria living in the soil. Animals get their nitrogen by eating plants or each other. When living things die, the return portion of the cycle begins. The dead remains are broken down, and because of even more bacteria, nitrogen finds its way back into the air. For humans the nitrogen cycle is very important because it affects how well plants grow. Some plants have their own nitrogen supply, thanks to nitrogen-fixing bacteria that live in their roots. These plants—such as clover, peas, and beans—have been grown for generations as a way of improving the fertility of the soil. Today nitrogen is also fixed industrially in order to make synthetic fertilizer.

Evolution

How many types of living things are there on Earth? Three hundred years ago, when scientists first began asking this question, they thought that the total was less than 10,000. Today we know that this is a huge underestimate. Almost two million different species have already been identified, and it is possible that ten times that number are still waiting to be discovered. This amazing richness has occurred through evolution—a process that allows living things to adapt gradually to different ways of life.

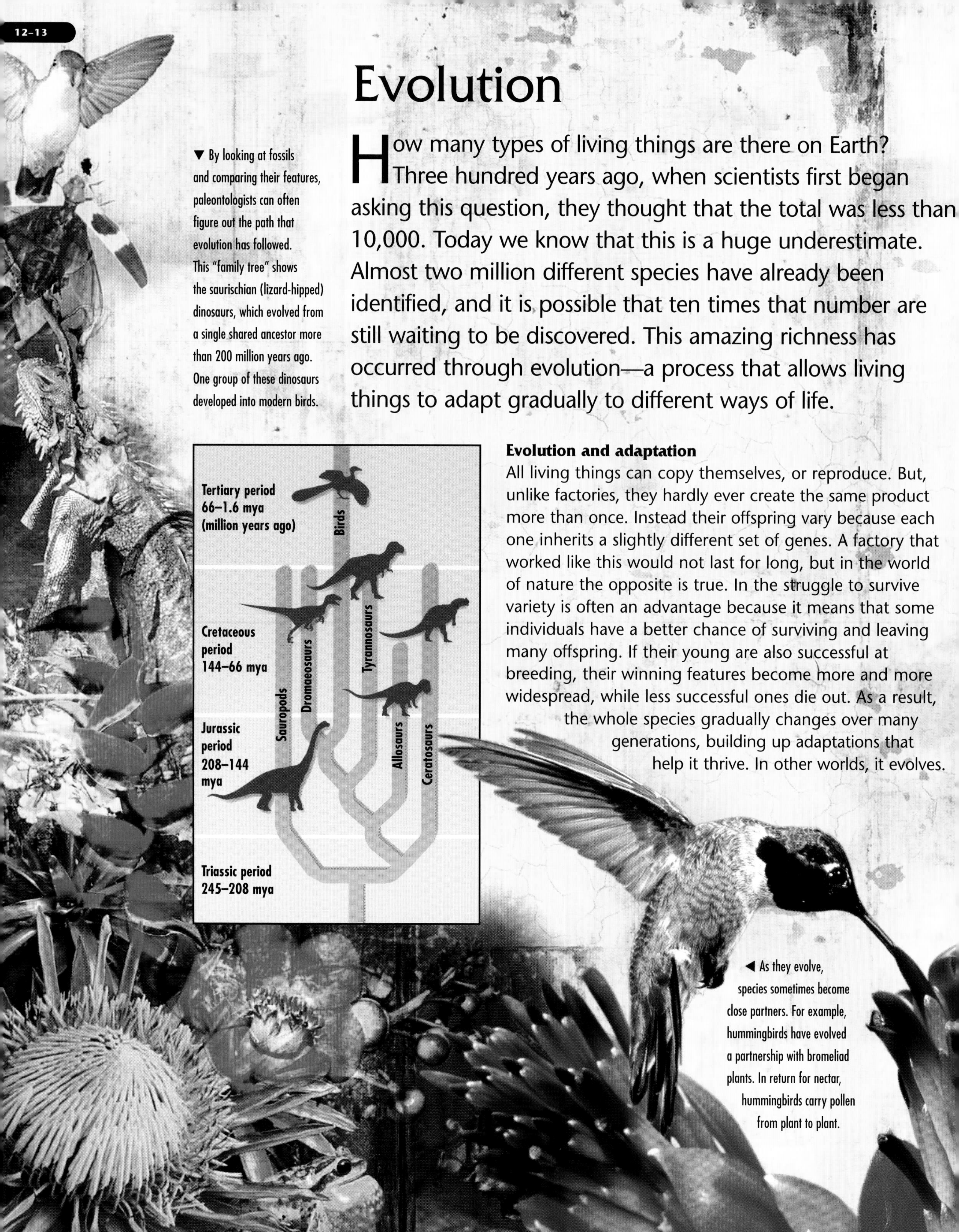

▼ By looking at fossils and comparing their features, paleontologists can often figure out the path that evolution has followed. This "family tree" shows the saurischian (lizard-hipped) dinosaurs, which evolved from a single shared ancestor more than 200 million years ago. One group of these dinosaurs developed into modern birds.

Evolution and adaptation

All living things can copy themselves, or reproduce. But, unlike factories, they hardly ever create the same product more than once. Instead their offspring vary because each one inherits a slightly different set of genes. A factory that worked like this would not last for long, but in the world of nature the opposite is true. In the struggle to survive variety is often an advantage because it means that some individuals have a better chance of surviving and leaving many offspring. If their young are also successful at breeding, their winning features become more and more widespread, while less successful ones die out. As a result, the whole species gradually changes over many generations, building up adaptations that help it thrive. In other worlds, it evolves.

◀ As they evolve, species sometimes become close partners. For example, hummingbirds have evolved a partnership with bromeliad plants. In return for nectar, hummingbirds carry pollen from plant to plant.

The life and death of species

If you think of life as a bush, species are the tips of its twigs. Since life first appeared the bush has kept expanding because many new species have evolved. The bush also has many dead-end branches, however, where species have become extinct. Extinction is a natural process that usually happens gradually, but occasionally natural catastrophes have swept away thousands of species at one time. The last of these mass extinctions occurred 66 million years ago at the end of the dinosaur age (see page 17).

Measuring biodiversity

Evolution works so slowly that losing species is a serious problem. Today the extinction rate is rising, so biologists are urgently counting the species that we have. So far around 4,500 types of mammals and 9,500 birds have been identified. These groups of animals have been well studied, so it is unlikely that many more will be found. But with some groups, such as insects and deep-sea fish, the work has only just begun. If the extinction rate keeps climbing, many species could die out before they are discovered.

Biodiversity hot spots

In some places, called biodiversity hot spots, evolution seems to have gone into overdrive. They contain a richness of life that is out of all proportion to their size. For example, South Africa's Cape of Good Hope (Cape Province) is home to an astounding 8,000 species of plants, two thirds of which live nowhere else. Brazil's Atlantic Forest is a hot spot for plants and monkeys, while Madagascar has five families of primates that are unique to that part of the world.

▶ This map shows the world's biodiversity hot spots—regions that have an unusually rich variety of species, including many that live nowhere else. Many hot spots have been damaged by human activities, which makes it even more important to protect the areas that remain.

▲ Suspended from a hot-air balloon, an inflatable sled allows biologists to examine the rain forest canopy as they search for undiscovered species. These scientists are working in Gabon—a central African country that still contains large areas of unspoiled forests.

Homes and habitats

Even without modern technology, humans can survive in mountains, deserts, and on land close to the poles. With technology, we can endure some very hostile environments such as the deep sea or space. But we are an exception. Unlike us, most of the world's living things have adapted for survival in only one habitat. This type of specialization helps shape the global map of life.

Habitats

Habitats include a variety of different surroundings, from open grasslands to seafloor mud. Unlike a home, a habitat normally supplies all the resources that a living thing needs. This does not mean just the obvious things, such as space, food, and daylight, but also some obscure ones such as the level of rare minerals in the soil. An ideal habitat for one species can be less than ideal for others. For example, some bacteria flourish in hot springs that contain diluted sulfuric acid. In this extreme habitat any fish would quickly dissolve.

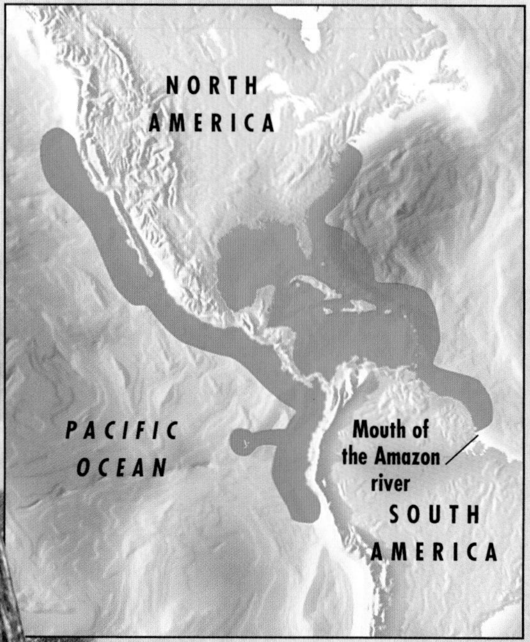

NORTH AMERICA

PACIFIC OCEAN

Mouth of the Amazon river

SOUTH AMERICA

◀ ▲ Brown pelicans live in a coastal habitat (shown in orange). On South America's east coast they do not live farther south than the mouth of the Amazon river because there the mud-filled water prevents them from spotting food.

A place on the map

Because hot springs always occur in volcanic regions, this is the only place where acid-proof bacteria are found. In the same way the distribution of other species is determined by the conditions that they need. For example, brown pelicans feed by dive-bombing fish, so they must have clear water in order to see their prey. Avocets, on the other hand, have beaks with sensitive tips, so these birds can feed in water that is as cloudy as a cup of tea with milk. Sometimes the distribution of one species controls the distribution of another. Robber crabs feed mostly on coconuts, so they are found only in parts of the tropics where coconuts grow. On an even bigger scale coral reefs are found only in warm-water regions, so all the animals that depend on coral need warm water too.

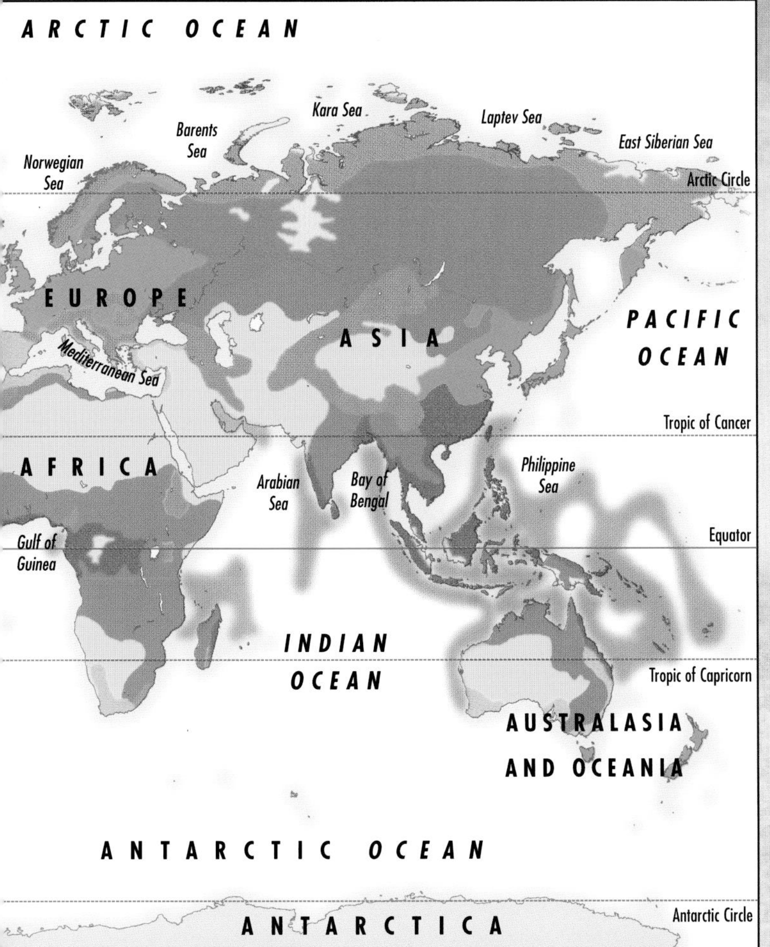

Biomes

Despite its local differences, life shows many similarities around the world. African rain forests look very similar to Asian rain forests, even though they contain different animals and plants. In the same way American grasslands have a lot in common with Australian grasslands, even though they are on opposite sides of the planet. These worldwide mixtures of plants and animals are known as biomes; unlike habitats, they are big and clear enough to be visible from space. After biomes there is only one more step up in size, to the biosphere—the complete collection of every place where living things are found.

◀ This map shows all the major biomes of the world, as they were before humans started to clear land for farming. Biomes are shaped mostly by climate because this affects the type of plants that can grow in any particular place.

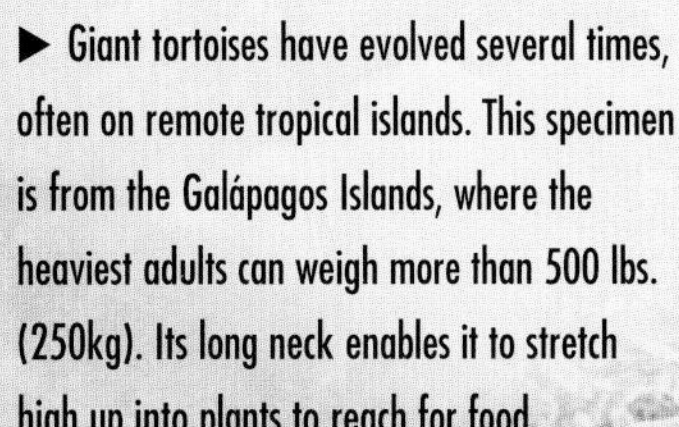

▶ Giant tortoises have evolved several times, often on remote tropical islands. This specimen is from the Galápagos Islands, where the heaviest adults can weigh more than 500 lbs. (250kg). Its long neck enables it to stretch high up into plants to reach for food.

Local specialties

Many habitat types are scattered across the globe, so you might expect their inhabitants to be worldwide as well. A few species—such as the barn owl—are truly global, but most are linked to a specific part of the planet. Giant tortoises live on volcanic slopes in the Galápagos Islands but not on the same type of slopes in South America, 500 mi. (800km) away. The reason for this is that every species originally evolves in one place. Some manage to spread far from their birthplace, but many are closed in by barriers such as mountains or the sea. These obstacles divide the world into separate regions, each with species that are found there and nowhere else. Remote islands—such as the Galápagos and New Zealand—are especially rich in these "endemic" species. Unfortunately, endemic species often suffer when foreign plants and animals are introduced.

▶ Spinifex grassland covers most of the Australian outback. This drought-resistant plant grows in scattered clumps, which provide shelter and food for animals. One bird—the spinifex pigeon—is almost always found where this grass grows.

▲ In Arizona's Petrified Forest fossilized tree trunks are scattered across the desert floor. These remains show that the climate there was once much more humid than it is today.

Coping with change

It is hard to imagine anything more delicate than a butterfly as it flutters from flower to flower or something more helpless than an antelope being stalked by a pride of lions. But simply by existing, creatures like this prove that they are a lot tougher than they seem. Like all living things, their ancestors adapted to a changing world, and they do the same when they breed and pass on their genes. But today's species also have to cope with something new: worldwide changes caused by human beings.

An unpredictable world

Earth is always changing in different ways. Some changes follow predictable rhythms. These rhythms include the shifting seasons, the tides, and the 24-hour cycle of night and day. But even bigger changes are also taking place. Continents creep across the planet's surface, ice ages come and go, and sea levels rise and fall. Unlike seasons, these do not follow a clear-cut pattern, so no one can predict exactly where they are heading. For living things these changes can be a problem, but they open up new opportunities too.

Continental drift

Earth's outer crust is cool, but a huge amount of heat is trapped in its core. This heat causes volcanoes and earthquakes, and it keeps all the continents moving. Continental drift is an incredibly slow process: the fastest mover—South America—travels at less than 0.8 in. (20cm) each year. But, over millions of years, this movement transforms the planet's surface, splitting and joining continents and the wildlife found there. Continental drift is an important force in evolution because it separates groups of plants or animals, giving them a chance to develop in different ways.

Climate change

Scientists know how continents move, but long-term climate change is harder to explain. Ice ages may be triggered by changes in Earth's orbit or by clouds of dust that volcanoes eject into the air. Continental drift could also play a part by blocking warm sea currents that carry heat toward the poles. Whatever the cause, these swings in climate can be dramatic. At the height of the last ice age, 18,000 years ago, ice sheets spread as far as southern England. Today, on the other hand, most of the world's glaciers are shrinking fast.

◀ Between 1980 (far left) and 2002 (left) Peru's Jacabamba glacier melted and receded as the world's climate warmed. The climate has often warmed up in the past, through natural changes, but this time human activities seem to be the cause.

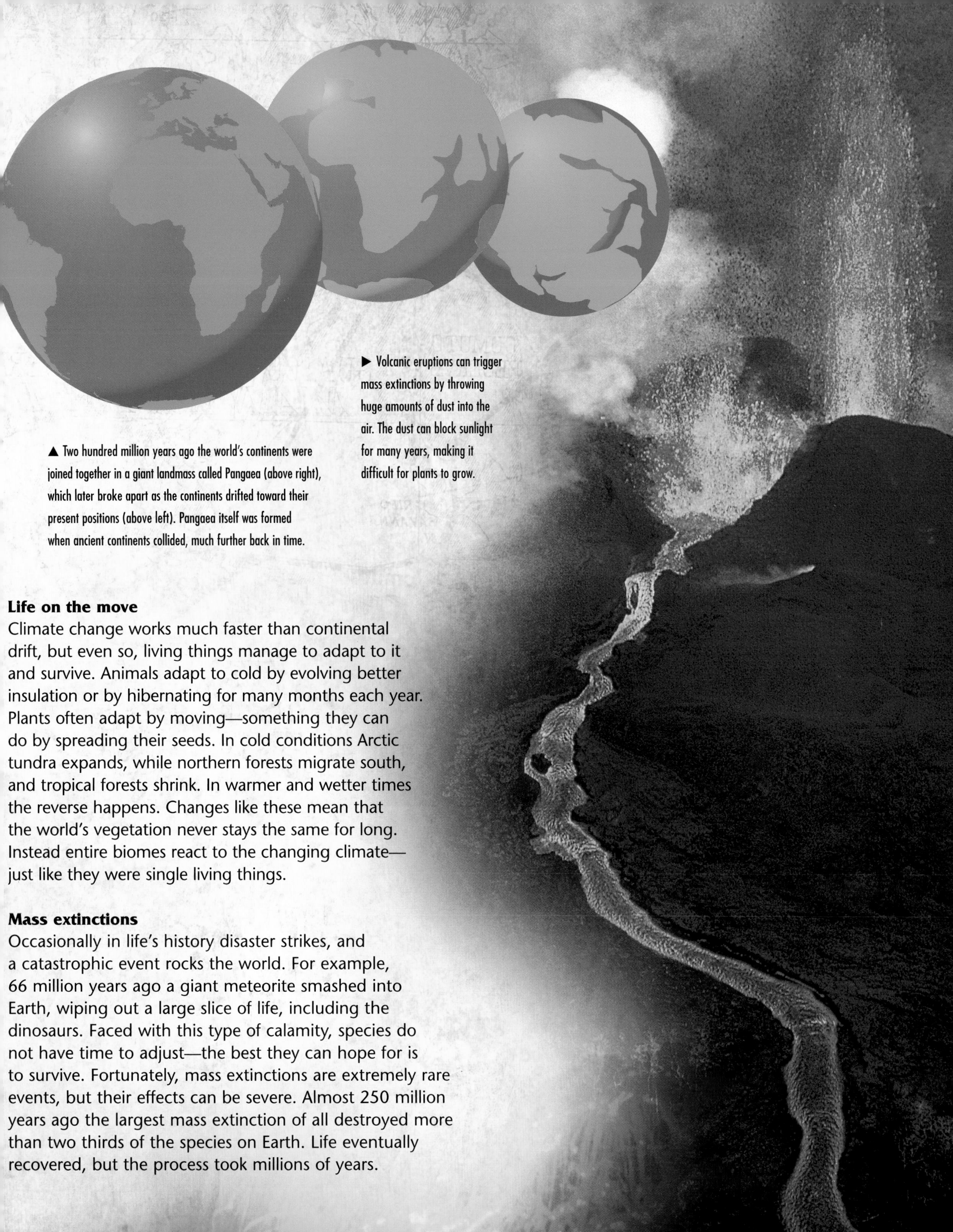

▲ Two hundred million years ago the world's continents were joined together in a giant landmass called Pangaea (above right), which later broke apart as the continents drifted toward their present positions (above left). Pangaea itself was formed when ancient continents collided, much further back in time.

▶ Volcanic eruptions can trigger mass extinctions by throwing huge amounts of dust into the air. The dust can block sunlight for many years, making it difficult for plants to grow.

Life on the move

Climate change works much faster than continental drift, but even so, living things manage to adapt to it and survive. Animals adapt to cold by evolving better insulation or by hibernating for many months each year. Plants often adapt by moving—something they can do by spreading their seeds. In cold conditions Arctic tundra expands, while northern forests migrate south, and tropical forests shrink. In warmer and wetter times the reverse happens. Changes like these mean that the world's vegetation never stays the same for long. Instead entire biomes react to the changing climate—just like they were single living things.

Mass extinctions

Occasionally in life's history disaster strikes, and a catastrophic event rocks the world. For example, 66 million years ago a giant meteorite smashed into Earth, wiping out a large slice of life, including the dinosaurs. Faced with this type of calamity, species do not have time to adjust—the best they can hope for is to survive. Fortunately, mass extinctions are extremely rare events, but their effects can be severe. Almost 250 million years ago the largest mass extinction of all destroyed more than two thirds of the species on Earth. Life eventually recovered, but the process took millions of years.

SUMMARY OF CHAPTER 1: FRAGILE EARTH

Conditions for life

This chapter looked at one of the most important questions in science: why does life exist on our planet but nowhere else that we know of? The answer is that Earth had the right mix of conditions for life to appear: it is the right distance from the Sun, it has a protective atmosphere, and most of the planet's surface is covered by water. Once life began, it managed to adapt and evolve, and it has been doing this successfully for almost four billion years. Life may exist elsewhere—Mars seems to be the most likely place—but it has not yet been found.

The biosphere

Although Earth is huge, only a small fraction of the planet—known as the biosphere—is actually home to living things.

Giant tortoise, Galápagos Islands

In the biosphere the Sun's energy provides the driving force that keeps living things alive. It also provides the energy that keeps carbon and other vital substances on the move. The only things that use sunlight directly are plants—through a process called photosynthesis—and some specialized bacteria. Animals get their energy indirectly by eating plants or other living things.

Patterns of life

Over long periods of time living things slowly change, or evolve. Evolution does not happen in a single lifetime. Instead it occurs over many generations as each species adapts to its surroundings. During evolution new species sometimes develop, and existing ones eventually become extinct. Evolution allows living things to cope with long-term changes such as ice ages and continental drift. It also creates biomes—the characteristic mixtures of plants and animals that exist all over the world. On rare occasions, however, large slices of Earth's life have been wiped out by cataclysmic natural events such as meteorite strikes and enormous volcanic eruptions.

Go further . . .

Take a trip through Earth's history by visiting this online time machine: www.ucmp.berkeley.edu/help/timeform.html

Discover up-to-date information about the search for extraterrestrial life at: www.seti.org

Find out more about the world's biodiversity hot spots by exploring this interactive map: www.biodiversityhotspots.org/xp/Hotspots/home/interactive_map.xml

The Kingfisher Book of Evolution by Stephen Webster (Kingfisher, 2000)

Atlas of the Prehistoric World by Douglas Palmer (Discovery Books, 1999)

Biologist

Studies living things and the way that they work.

Ecologist

Examines the connections between different types of living things and the environments in which they live.

Exobiologist

Studies the origin of life and its possible existence on other planets.

Glaciologist

Examines ice and frozen landscapes and the effects of ice ages in the past.

Paleontologist

Investigates prehistoric life by examining fossils that living things have left behind.

Visit the American Museum of Natural History in New York City, where permanent exhibitions, including the famous dinosaur halls, explore how life has evolved over time.

American Museum of Natural History
Central Park West at 79th Street
New York, NY 10024-5191
Phone: (212) 769-5192
www.amnh.org

Find out more about different environments—from rain forests to deserts—at the "Living With the Land" attraction at Epcot Center.

Walt Disney World Resort
Orlando, FL 32480
Phone: (407) 828-1000
http://disneyworld.disney.go.com

Flooded village, Tana river valley, Kenya

CHAPTER 2

Planet under pressure

Five hundred years ago European explorers completed the first-ever around-the-world voyage. It took three years. Today jet planes circle Earth in one thousandth of that time. Satellites can take less than one hour. These comparisons show something we are all becoming aware of: Earth is a relatively small planet, and our impact on it is growing. Because of our booming population and advances in science, we are starting to affect the way the entire world works. Part of our impact comes from the resources that we use such as energy, water, and space. The more we take, the less there is for other living things. Just as important is the waste we produce, from household garbage to car exhaust fumes. Some of this stays close to home, but some travels through the oceans and the atmosphere—where it can have far-reaching effects.

An escalating impact

Five hundred thousand years ago, when our species first appeared, the human population was small, and people had very little impact on the planet. But since then three major breakthroughs have dramatically increased our effects on the world around us. The first was the agricultural revolution, which took place around 10,000 years ago, when people first learned how to farm. The second was the industrial revolution, which began in the early 1700s, while the third—the information revolution—is happening now.

▶ Lined up in the New Mexican desert, this bank of radio telescopes can probe deep into space. Because of instruments like these, we know much more about the universe than people did 50 years ago, and we have surveyed the entire solar system in amazing detail. But despite these extraordinary advances, technology has failed to solve many of the problems that we face back home on Earth.

◀ In Madagascar, like in other developing countries, most people still directly depend on farming for their survival. This woman is winnowing rice—a task that involves separating the edible grains from the unwanted husks. Over time Madagascar's farmers have transformed their island home, clearing forests and replacing them with a patchwork of pastures and fields. It is a change that has also happened in many other parts of the world.

The agricultural revolution

For most of human history people lived by hunting and collecting food from the wild. To find enough to eat, they had to keep moving. But around 10,000 years ago a new type of lifestyle began to appear as people discovered how to grow crops and raise animals for food. Farming meant that they could settle down in one place, and it generated surplus food that could be stored and traded. This revolutionary way of life had some far-reaching effects. It allowed towns and cities to develop, and it also transformed the countryside around these places. With a more reliable food supply, the human population began to grow.

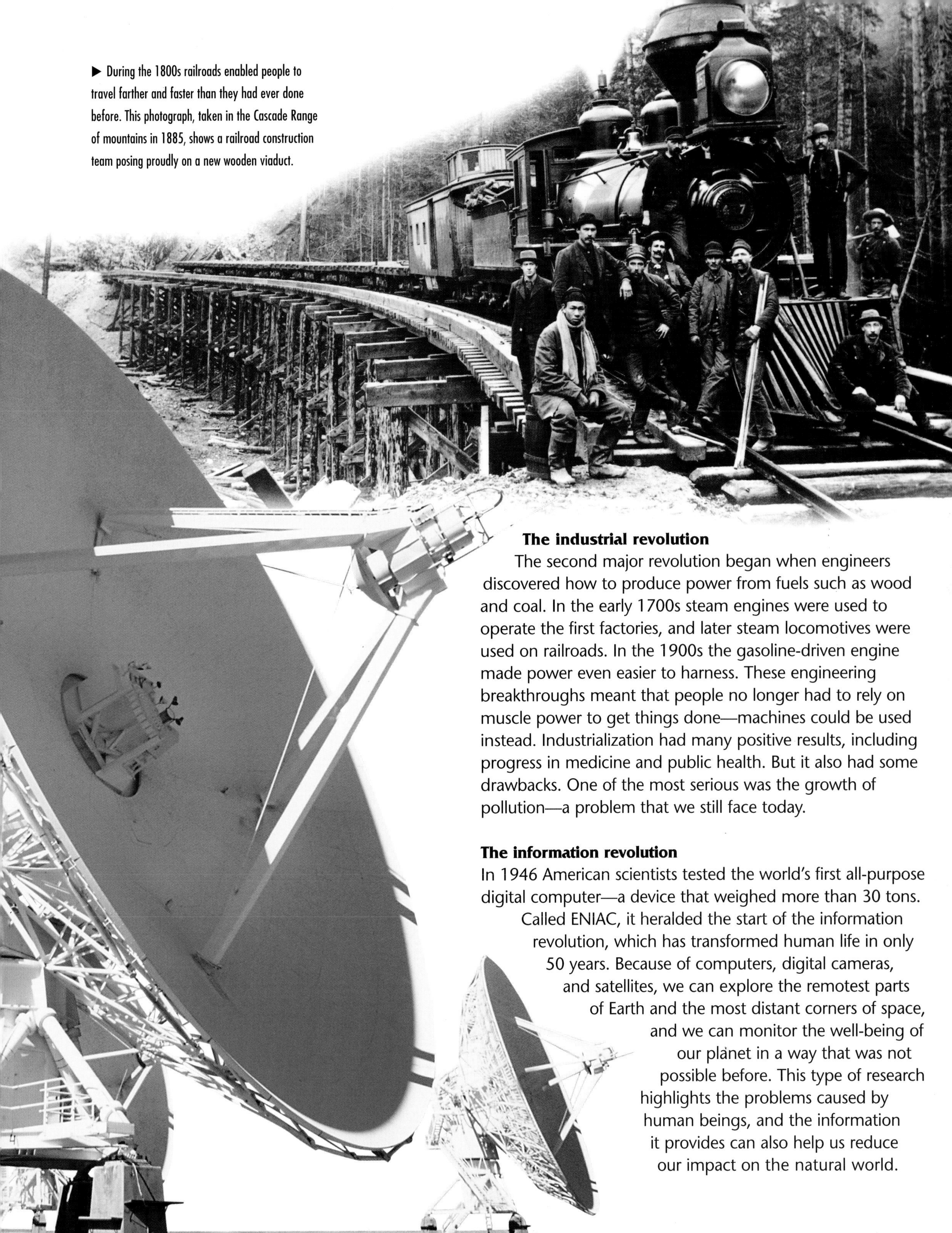

▶ During the 1800s railroads enabled people to travel farther and faster than they had ever done before. This photograph, taken in the Cascade Range of mountains in 1885, shows a railroad construction team posing proudly on a new wooden viaduct.

The industrial revolution

The second major revolution began when engineers discovered how to produce power from fuels such as wood and coal. In the early 1700s steam engines were used to operate the first factories, and later steam locomotives were used on railroads. In the 1900s the gasoline-driven engine made power even easier to harness. These engineering breakthroughs meant that people no longer had to rely on muscle power to get things done—machines could be used instead. Industrialization had many positive results, including progress in medicine and public health. But it also had some drawbacks. One of the most serious was the growth of pollution—a problem that we still face today.

The information revolution

In 1946 American scientists tested the world's first all-purpose digital computer—a device that weighed more than 30 tons. Called ENIAC, it heralded the start of the information revolution, which has transformed human life in only 50 years. Because of computers, digital cameras, and satellites, we can explore the remotest parts of Earth and the most distant corners of space, and we can monitor the well-being of our planet in a way that was not possible before. This type of research highlights the problems caused by human beings, and the information it provides can also help us reduce our impact on the natural world.

Population growth

Every day the world's population grows by around 200,000 people. There are now more than three times as many people as there were 100 years ago, and today's figure could double by 2100. This increase is mainly owing to progress in public health, which means that more people survive childhood to have children themselves. For the human species it is an astonishing achievement, but our booming population creates problems for us—and for the rest of the living world.

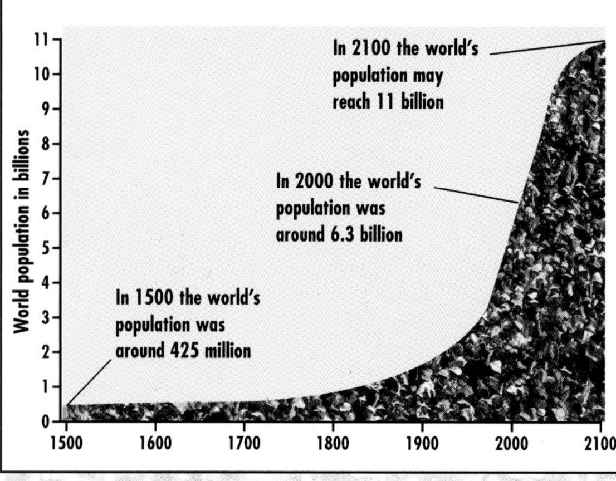

▲ This graph shows how the world's population has grown in the last 500 years, and it also looks ahead to the start of the 2100s. At some point in the future the population will stop growing, but no one knows for sure when this will happen.

Takeoff

Until the late 1700s the human population grew slowly because many people died from diseases such as smallpox. But after the discovery of vaccinations and improvements in sanitation childhood deaths fell dramatically, and the population began to boom. This burst of growth began in the industrialized countries of North America and western Europe, and from there it spread across the world.

▼ A Kenyan boy is vaccinated against diphtheria, polio, and tetanus—diseases that once killed millions of children around the world. Like many developing countries, Kenya's population is booming, due to better medical care.

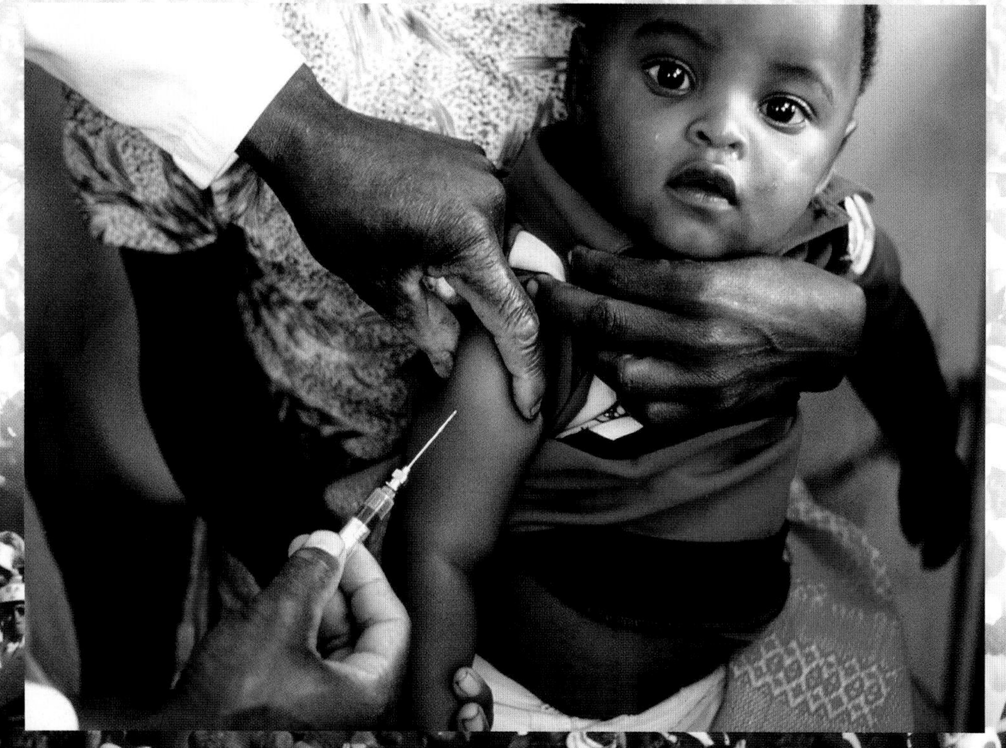

Making the transition

The world's population is rising, but there are big differences in population growth across the globe. In many European countries women have an average of less than two children, which is the number needed to keep the population steady. The population of these countries will fall unless extra people arrive from outside. In many African nations, however, the average is more than five children, so the population is climbing sharply. But Europe was once like this too. Through a process called the demographic transition, European family sizes have shrunk. Experts predict that, sooner or later, developing countries will also experience this transition.

Closing the gap

In Europe and North America the demographic transition took several generations to complete. But in some of today's developing countries birth control programs have helped speed it up. India, for example, launched family planning programs in the 1950s, while China adopted a policy of "one child per family" in 1979. These measures are controversial, especially when they involve tough penalties for breaking the rules. But they have had the desired effect. Without them, countries like China would have millions of extra people to feed.

▶ A Chinese billboard from the 1980s explains the benefits of having just one child in each family. Over 20 years this drastic population control policy reduced the number of births by around 230 million—almost four times the entire population of Great Britain.

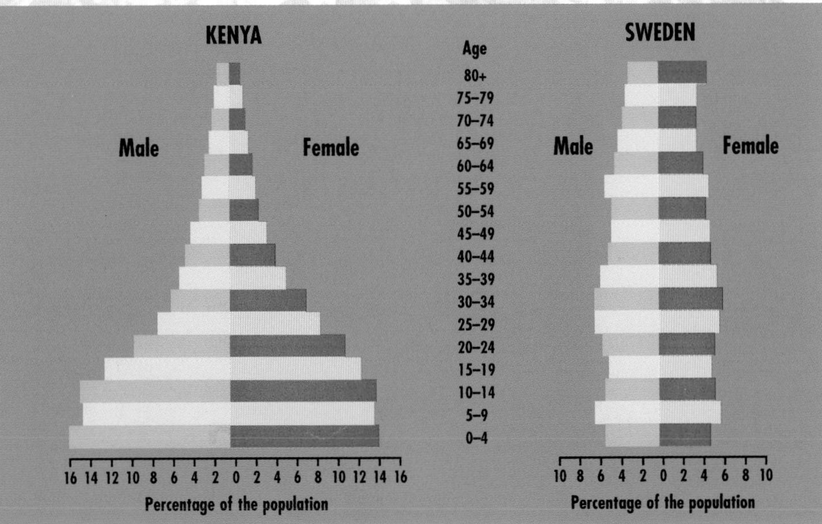

▲ This "age pyramid" divides Kenya's population according to people's ages. There are many more young people than old people—a sign that the population is booming.

▲ Sweden's age pyramid looks very different from Kenya's. The age groups are almost balanced, showing that the population is stable. In Sweden many more people survive into their 70s and 80s.

Joining the ranks

Thirty years ago many scientists believed that the human population was running out of control. Looking forward to the year 2000, some foresaw bleak prospects for an overloaded planet. Their predictions have not come true, but our world is certainly feeling the strain. Many environmental problems are directly linked to population, so the more of us there are, the harder they are to prevent. The good news is that human numbers look like they will eventually reach a peak, and after that they may even fall. The bad news is that all the extra people will want food, space, and consumer goods, creating further problems for the natural world.

Habitat destruction

The more people there are on Earth, the more land they need. This simple fact lies at the heart of habitat destruction, a worldwide problem that is eating away at the natural world. Some habitats are destroyed to make space for farmland, while others are buried by buildings or roads. The quest for resources also damages habitats—especially when the search involves timber, minerals, or oil.

Quarrying and mining

Bricks, concrete, windows, and soda cans have one thing in common—they are all produced by quarrying or mining. So is coal, as well as the crushed stone that is used to build roads. Life without these materials would be hard, but getting access to them can have damaging effects on the living world. Quarries and mines obliterate habitats—either by digging them up or by smothering them under piles of waste.

Vanishing wetlands

Beneath swamps and salt marshes is some of the most fertile soil on Earth. This helps explain why so many of the world's wetlands have been drained and turned into fields. In the U.S. more than half of the nation's wetlands have disappeared since 1800, and the remainder are shrinking fast. Healthy wetlands play a useful role in controlling floods and purifying water, and they are rich in wildlife. But when wetlands vanish, their wildlife also disappears.

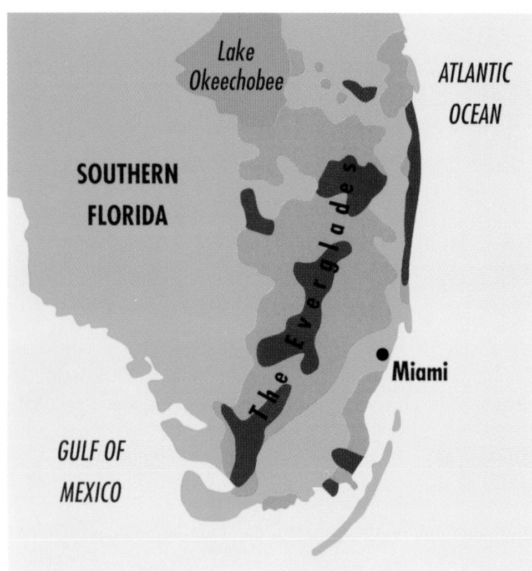

KEY TO MAP

Permanently flooded land, 1900

Permanently flooded land, today

◀ ▼ The Florida Everglades is the wetland home of more than one dozen endangered species of animals, including the snail (Everglade) kite and the American crocodile. Before humans began to drain the area the Everglades was like a huge sheet of water flowing gently toward the sea. Today canals and pipelines divert much of this water to farms and towns, and only isolated pockets of swamps stay flooded all year round.

▲ Healthy coral reefs (left) teem with life, making them perfect places for fishing. But when fishermen use dynamite to stun their catch, the coral is often killed. When the coral dies, the reef soon disintegrates (right).

Offshore damage

Land habitats have always been hit hardest by our need for space and food. But in the last 50 years habitat destruction has also spread offshore. Fishing boats trawl their nets over the seabed, scraping up plants and animals and creating long-lasting scars. Coral reefs are affected by overfishing and by sediment that is washed off of the land—especially from towns and farms. An even more serious problem is global warming, which can make coral get sick and die. Faced with all of these threats, many of the world's coral reefs are already in trouble.

Deforestation

Forests are the richest habitats on land and are also some of the most threatened. Since farming began more than half of the world's tree cover has been cleared to make space for fields. In some places—such as Europe—deforestation took place long ago, but in the tropics it began much more recently and is happening at record-breaking speed. Tropical forests are cleared for farms and also for their timber—a single trunk can be worth as much as $5,000.

The loss of tropical forests is a disaster for wildlife. More than one third of the world's birds rely on this habitat for survival, together with two thirds of all primates—animals that include monkeys and apes. Tropical forests are also the natural home of around half of the world's broad-leaved trees. As forests become smaller and are crisscrossed by roads, all of these species face a tough fight for survival.

◀ The Bingham Canyon copper mine in Utah is the largest mine in the world. In giant mines like this the metal content of the rock is often as low as five percent. For every pound of metal that is recovered 42 lbs. (19kg) of polluting waste has to be dug up, processed, and dumped.

Growing food

Farmland is essential to our survival. Today's crops yield much better harvests than ones 50 years ago, but with a growing population there is pressure to produce even more. This is a tough challenge because farmland needs to be kept in good condition so that it can keep producing food year after year. If things go wrong, the results can be disastrous—crops can fail, and the soil may even disappear.

Intensive farming

To produce good yields, crops need fertile soil. Traditionally, farmers fertilized soil by adding animal manure—a technique that organic farmers still use today. But in 1909 Fritz Haber (1868–1934), a German chemist, devised a way of making artificial fertilizer. Haber's invention launched intensive farming—a type of agriculture that relies on artificial inputs such as fertilizers, pesticides, fuel, and animal feed. Intensive farming has increased world food production dramatically—but at a price—it uses a lot of energy, and its chemicals often contaminate soil, water, and food.

◀ During the "dust bowl" years in the 1930s billions of tons of soil blew off farmland in the Midwest. This ecological disaster was created by droughts and poor farming practices. In some parts of the world today soil is disappearing more than 10,000 times faster than it is being made.

Soil erosion

In natural habitats the remains of dead plants break down to form soil, and the roots of living plants hold the soil in place. But when the ground is cleared and plowed, the soil can be washed away by rain or blown away by wind. Soil erosion is a big problem for farmers because new soil forms very slowly—often at a rate of less than .04 in. (1mm) per year.

▲ Around one third of the world's land surface is used for farming. Above, an intensively farmed field of corn is being harvested to make animal feed.

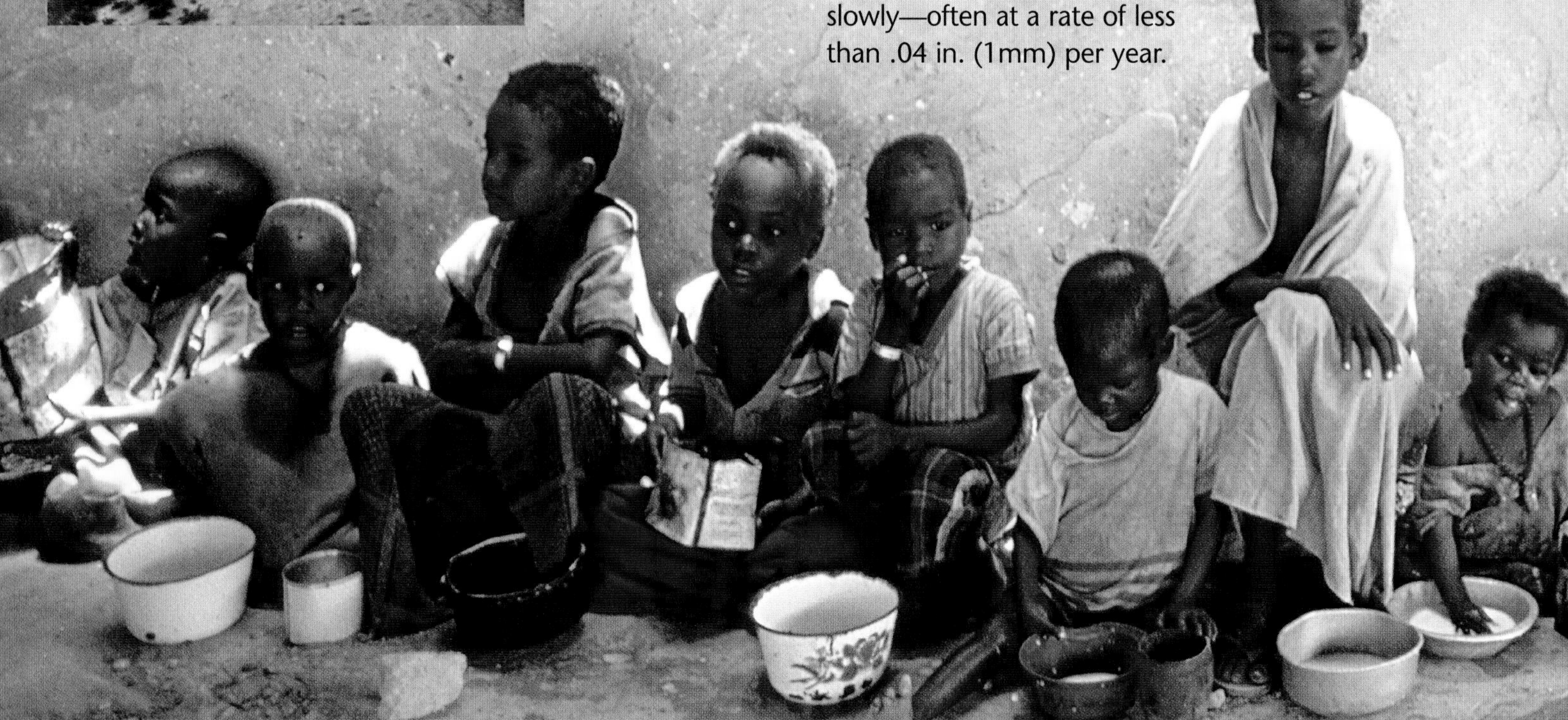

▶ Planes swoop over a field in Texas, dusting a crop with pesticides. Each field may be treated with more than one dozen different chemicals before the crop is ready to be harvested.

Feeding the world

Despite the surge in the human population, the world's farmland still produces enough food to keep everyone on the planet well fed. This has been achieved by clearing more land, by making farming more intensive, and by breeding better strains of crops. However, three fourths of the world's people—mainly in Africa and Asia—have less food than they need. The reason for this is that food supplies are unevenly spread. Developed regions, such as North America and Europe, produce more food than they can consume, while poorer parts of the world go short. In these areas farmers do not have enough money to buy improved seeds and tools, and climatic hazards—such as droughts and floods—often make a difficult situation even worse. Emergency food aid can prevent people from starving, but the real solution to hunger is to help farmers get the most from their land.

Farming and wildlife

Until the 1950s fields often teemed with colorful weeds, and farmland birds could rely on plentiful seeds and insects. Some organic farms are still like this, but intensive farmland is very different. Herbicides and pesticides keep weeds and insects at bay, while combines gather up every speck of grain. Hedges and trees are often cleared away to make larger fields, leaving wild animals with nowhere to breed. These changes help farms produce food more efficiently, with fewer losses from pests and diseases. The downside is that wild plants and animals find themselves squeezed out.

▼ These hungry children are eating a much-needed meal at a relief center in Somalia. In this part of eastern Africa a long civil war has made it difficult for farmers to grow food.

Expanding cities

If you live in North America or Europe, there is a 75 percent chance that your home is in a town or a city, instead of in the countryside. If you live in Australia or Japan, the likelihood is even greater. In the near future more than half of the world's population will live in urban surroundings—an enormous change from the days when most people's homes were on or close to farmland. Urban living has a huge impact on the natural world because almost everything that people need has to be brought in from outside.

▼ Most people dream about owning their own home. This picture, taken in Texas, shows what happens when this dream comes true—wide belts of newly built houses spread across the countryside.

Cities and megacities

In 1800 only one city in the world—Beijing, China—had more than one million inhabitants. At that time most people had never been to a city, and they had no real idea of what urban life was like. Since then the world's cities have grown at an amazing rate. China alone has more than 70 cities with one-million-plus people, and the world's largest cities have shot past the 15-million mark. These "megacities" include São Paulo, Brazil, Mumbai, India, and Tokyo, Japan, which sprawl over hundreds of square miles of land. Each one is swelling by thousands of people every day, so counting their populations is an almost impossible task.

▲ Mexico City is home to almost 21 million people. With around three million cars, the city's traffic jams are notorious, and air pollution is a serious health hazard.

Why cities grow

Because the human population is rising fast, cities grow too. But another change is also fueling urban growth. Before the industrial revolution (see page 21) most people worked on the land, and in the least developed countries many still do. But when countries become industrialized, there are more jobs in cities than in the countryside, and people begin to move. This is happening in China, southern Asia, and Latin America—three regions with the fastest-growing cities in the world.

▶ Mumbai, or Bombay, is the largest city in India and is also its leading port. It is a place of stark contrasts, with a thriving commercial center and luxury hotels but also shantytowns made up of rough, homemade shacks that let in the monsoon rains.

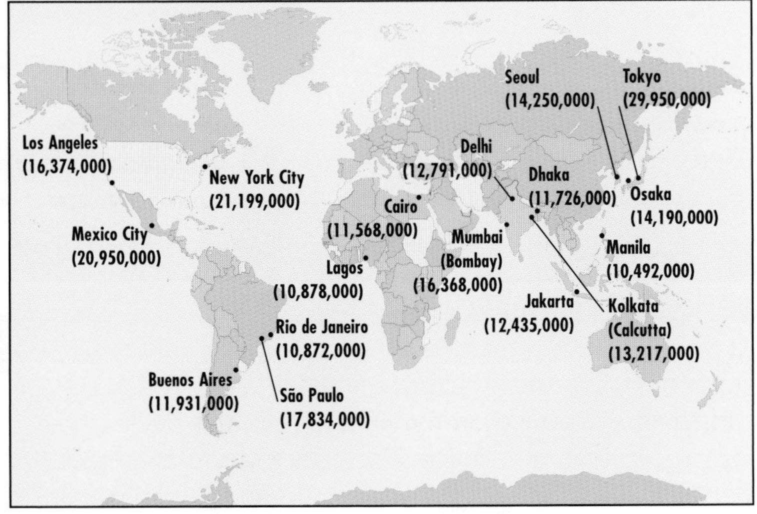

▲ In 2002 17 cities had populations of more than ten million people. In developing countries most cities are still growing quickly, but in North America and western Europe many have stopped expanding because people have started moving to smaller towns.

Living on the edge
When a city's population grows gradually, houses and services can be planned in advance. But in many developing nations resources are scarce, and housing can be hard to find. So the poorest city dwellers are forced to build their own homes using whatever they can find on hand. On the outskirts of cities such as Rio de Janeiro, Brazil, Cape Town, South Africa, and Mumbai, India, makeshift houses are crowded together in shantytowns. Life there can be extremely tough. Few shantytowns have an actual water supply or sanitation system, and good jobs are rare.

Spreading suburbs
Unplanned housing often causes environmental problems, but so does housing in more prosperous parts of the world. In these areas suburban houses spread into the countryside, destroying natural habitats. Because these houses each have their own garage and yard, they take up much more space than city-center homes. Spreading suburbs are a problem in crowded countries, such as Great Britain, but they are also a headache in North America and Australia—places that are famous for their wide-open spaces. In the U.S. new suburbs swallow up almost 3,900 sq. mi. (10,000km^2) of land each year—or 12 times the area of central New York City.

▲ This overflowing trash can shows one of the reasons why we produce so much waste—food and drinks are sold in packages that are designed to be thrown away.

The age of waste

The next time you buy a take-out meal think about what happens to the packaging. It is only used once, but its lifetime may be as long as your own. Waste like this adds to the huge mountain of garbage that each of us throws away every year. Today waste is a global problem—one that reaches even the remotest parts of the world.

Changes in the trash

Human lifestyles have altered a lot in the past 100 years, and our garbage has changed as well. In 1900 there was very little packaging, and major purchases were built to last. Today packaging is everywhere, and the things we buy—from clothes to cell phones—soon become out-of-date or obsolete. In a world where shopping has become a major pastime, each of us generates up to one ton of household waste every year.

Getting rid of waste

Modern-day garbage contains large amounts of plastics—human-made materials that are very resistant to decay. Plastics are extremely useful, and it is hard to imagine life without them. But because bacteria and other microbes cannot break them down, they never completely disappear. Plastic objects often break apart, but the fragments that are left behind can last for hundreds of years.

Besides plastics, household and industrial waste contains countless different materials, all mixed together. Disposing of it safely is not easy. The traditional solution—burying it in landfill sites—causes problems because garbage decomposes underground. It can give off hazardous gases, as well as liquids that can trickle into rivers. An alternative is to burn it in special incinerators; the heat can even be used to generate electric power. But incinerators are controversial because they release dangerous pollutants into the air.

▲ Many of the world's beaches are littered with waste, even though it is illegal for ships to dump garbage at sea.

Garbage at sea

Seawater is always on the move, so it spreads garbage far and wide. Waste can drift across the oceans, and even remote islands collect garbage on their shores. In the 1990s a beach survey was carried out on Ducie Island, which is uninhabited by humans. Despite being one of the world's most isolated spots, 2,790 mi. (4,500km) off the coast of South America, hundreds of pieces of garbage were found, from plastic toys to gas cylinders. Drifting waste is not just an eyesore—it is a menace to many sea animals. Discarded ropes and nets can entangle seals and birds, both at sea and on the shore. Plastic bags may be swallowed by turtles and porpoises, which mistake them for jellyfish, their prey.

◀ After scavenging in a garbage dump this white stork has become tangled up in a plastic bag. Unless it can free itself, the stork's chances of survival are slim.

Waste and wildlife

Humans do not find garbage attractive, which is why we usually place it out of sight. But for many animals domestic waste holds the irresistible promise of food. Birds flock to landfill sites all over the world, and on city streets plastic garbage bags attract nocturnal scavengers such as foxes and raccoons. In Churchill, Canada, one waste site has even become a magnet for polar bears—repeat offenders have to be caught and removed by helicopters to prevent them from becoming a danger close to the town. None of these animals can change its behavior because nature has shaped them to eat whatever they find. But animals and human garbage are a dangerous mixture. Scavengers can drag away waste, scattering it and causing a health hazard. The animals are also at risk themselves because garbage is full of dangerous objects that can injure or even kill them.

▼ With so much waste to deal with, landfills can reach amazing sizes. Before it closed, New York City's main site, on Staten Island, covered almost 2,223 acres (equal to around 1,250 soccer fields), with mounds up to 197 ft. (60m) high.

Liquid assets

Water is one resource that everybody needs. But one in five people do not have access to safe drinking water, and in some parts of the world freshwater is becoming increasingly scarce. To make matters more complicated, water is often used as a cheap and easy way to dispose of waste. Water pollution creates problems for people and also for anything else living downstream.

▼ Industrial pollution kills water life and can contaminate drinking water supplies. The water gushing out of this pipe is obviously polluted, but some other types of water pollution are much harder to spot.

▼ Clean water is vital for good health. This Kenyan boy has access to clean water close to his home, but many people in developing countries have to use unsafe water—and they may face a long walk to find it.

Water on tap

Few of us stop to think about where water comes from when we turn on the faucet. In places with a damp climate household water is usually taken from rivers or lakes. Sometimes this surface water is piped hundreds of miles to places that are normally dry. But in most dry regions, such as Australia and the Midwest, water comes mainly from wells. This underground water trickles through microscopic spaces deep in the rocks, and it moves so slowly that it can be thousands of years old. Groundwater is a highly valuable resource, but like many others, it is being used a lot faster than it is being replaced.

A growing thirst

To stay alive, the average person needs less than 1 gal. (4L) of water per day, unless the climate is very hot. But where water is available at the turn of a faucet, most people use much more than this. Americans top the list, using around 60 gal. (230L) per day, while people in Europe and Japan are not far behind. But personal water consumption is only part of the story because farms and factories use water on a huge scale. When this amount is also included, the amount of water used per person often jumps by more than ten times.

When more means less

Our thirst for water can have a big impact on the natural world. One of Europe's largest wetlands, the Coto Doñana, in southern Spain, has shrunk by four fifths because so much water is being used for irrigation. And under the North American Great Plains one of the world's largest groundwater deposits, or aquifers, is shrinking fast for the same reason. Some experts think that it will be exhausted by 2040, leaving a vitally important grain-growing region running on an empty tank.

Water pollution

Water is good at dissolving things, which makes it ideal for disposing of waste. But if wastewater contaminates drinking supplies, many types of health problems can follow. In developed countries drinking water is often purified, and sewage is processed to reduce the chance of pollution. But this is an expensive job that many poorer countries cannot afford. As a result, around one billion people are forced to drink unsafe water, and at least five million people die each year from waterborne diseases. Wild animals also suffer, especially when water is polluted by chemicals from factories and farmland.

▲ Lake Powell is one of several artificial reservoirs on the Colorado river. So much water is withdrawn from these lakes—for use on farms and in cities—that the river sometimes dries up before it reaches the sea.

Unfair shares

In dry parts of the world water can be a source of disagreement—especially when someone takes more than their share. During the 1960s, for example, the government of the Soviet Union began a huge irrigation program in central Asia, using water that flowed into the Aral Sea. Today the Aral Sea has shrunk by more than half, leaving fishing boats high and dry. In the Middle East tensions related to water could have even more dangerous results. This region is desperately short of water, and its countries need more each year. If an agreement is not reached, the result could be a water war.

▼ A rusting fishing boat lies stranded on a dried-up shore of the Aral Sea. Forty years after its water started to be diverted for irrigation, this inland sea has been declared an ecological disaster zone.

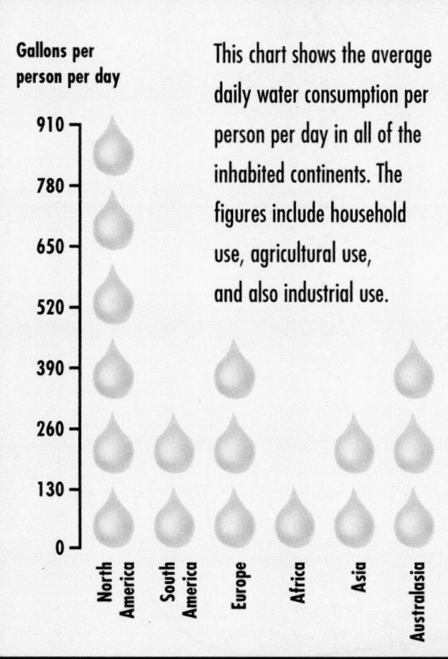

This chart shows the average daily water consumption per person per day in all of the inhabited continents. The figures include household use, agricultural use, and also industrial use.

Over the last 200 years the world's population has used more energy than the entire human race did in the previous 50,000 years. For most of us life becomes difficult if the electricity goes off, so it is hard to imagine what it would be like if we ran out of energy and the power never came back on. Fortunately, this is unlikely to happen, but our spiraling need for energy creates environmental problems that are proving difficult to solve. For a world addicted to energy this means some difficult choices now and in the years to come.

▼ Each year the world goes through more than three billion tons of oil. Producing this much oil is a huge and complicated operation, involving oil fields on land and offshore. This drilling rig stands off the north coast of Alaska in the shallow waters of the icy Beaufort Sea.

The big burn

Animals need energy to live, and they get this from their food. But long ago humans learned how to release extra energy by setting things on fire. At first this energy would have been difficult to use, but people gradually developed the technology to put it to work. Today energy keeps us warm, it carries information in computers and cell phones, and it powers aircraft as they crisscross the skies. There are many ways to obtain energy, but for most of our needs we still rely on the time-tested method of setting things on fire.

Fossil fuels

Wood is an important fuel in the developing world, but industrialized countries rely mostly on coal, natural gas, and oil. These are known as fossil fuels because they formed from the remains of plants that lived millions of years ago. These plants collected energy from sunlight, and the energy they stored is released when fossil fuels are burned. Coal supplies around one fourth of the world's energy, and natural gas supplies around one fifth. Oil comes out on top, at around 40 percent, because it is so convenient for powering things that move.

▼ During the 1970s two huge oil price rises triggered shortages and power cuts all over the Western world. Thirty years later the lights are on again, and we are burning up oil faster than ever before.

How long will fossil fuels last?

Of all the fossil fuels, coal is the only one that is not in danger of running out. Earth still contains billions of tons of unused coal reserves, which could last more than 500 years. Unfortunately, coal has many drawbacks as a fuel. It is difficult to dig, expensive to distribute, and it creates serious air pollution when it is burned. Natural gas is much cleaner, which is why many power plants have switched from coal to gas. There is a lot less of it, however, so today's "dash for gas" is unlikely to last for long. With oil, the future is complicated. New oil deposits are discovered every year, and new ways are found to get the most out of existing oil fields. But despite this, many experts think that we are closing in on the peak of oil production and that we will soon be heading for a decline. By the year 2050 oil will still be available, but it could be scarce. This means that it might be too expensive for many of the things we use it for today.

NATURAL GAS
World reserves: 120 billion tons
Rate of use: 1.9 billion tons per year
Time to depletion: around 60 years

OIL
World reserves: 140 billion tons
Rate of use: 3.2 billion tons per year
Time to depletion: around 45 years

NATURAL GAS
OIL
COAL
World reserves: 1.2 trillion tons
Rate of use: 2.2 billion tons per year
Time to depletion: around 550 years

◀ This chart shows our current reserves of the three fossil fuels, together with estimates of how long they are likely to last. Reserves sometimes go up when new deposits are found, but they can never be used completely. This is because the costs of extraction rise as a fuel becomes more scarce.

▲ Chernobyl nuclear power plant lies in ruins following a catastrophic explosion in April 1986. More than 200,000 people had to be evacuated from their homes—many have not been able to return.

The nuclear solution?

In the 1950s the U.S., Great Britain, and France began to generate electricity by using nuclear power. Unlike fossil fuels, the uranium fuel used in nuclear power plants does not burn. Instead its atoms split apart into lighter ones, releasing an enormous amount of energy. A coal-burning power plant uses several tons of fuel per minute, but a nuclear power plant can run on less than one ton of uranium per week. With this incredible potential, nuclear power once seemed to be the answer to the world's energy problems. Today we know differently. Because uranium fuel is highly radioactive, nuclear power plants need strict safety measures, and this makes them very expensive to build and to operate. Despite this, there have been a number of accidents—the worst, in the Ukrainian town of Chernobyl in 1986, created a radioactive cloud that covered a large part of Europe. This single disaster persuaded many governments that nuclear power is not worth the risk.

Air pollution

Water pollution is an age-old problem, but air pollution really began when people started burning fossil fuels. Eventually city air became so unhealthy that many countries had to tackle it through laws. Great Britain passed a Clean Air Act in 1956, and the U.S. did the same in 1963. These measures helped a lot, but air pollution has not gone away.

▼ After 100 years in polluted air this statue is being dissolved by acid rain. Acid rain attacks anything made of marble or limestone, and it can also corrode metals and bleach the color from paint. In cities and towns it causes damage costing billions of dollars per year.

Blowing in the wind

Unlike water, air is everywhere, and there is no danger of it running out. But fresh air is a different matter. Indoor air is often full of dust and man-made chemicals, while outdoor air contains gases and microscopic particles from factories, power plants, and vehicle exhausts. Some pollutants do not travel far because they quickly settle on the ground. Others can spread hundreds of miles downwind, affecting people and wildlife. A few stay in the atmosphere for many years—long enough for them to spread all over Earth.

Acid rain

In the 1980s strange things started happening in the forests of central Europe. Trees lost their leaves, and thousands of them slowly died. German scientists called it *Waldsterben*, or "forest death," and thought that it might be a new plant disease. But then a different culprit came to light—acid rain. Acid rain is produced when gases in smoke dissolve in droplets of airborne moisture. It looks and feels harmless, but it can kill trees and fish—and even eat through stone. Today acid rain affects many countries. Tall chimneys spread the problem, so the countryside is sometimes hit worse than places close to cities or towns.

◀ Around large cities pollution soars during rush hour, when bumper-to-bumper cars pump exhaust fumes into the air. Many cities now use automatic ozone detectors in order to track pollution levels and to warn people when it would be better not to drive.

Cars and smog

Car exhaust fumes contribute to acid rain, and they also contain poisonous gases, such as carbon monoxide and ozone, and tiny particles of soot that can travel deep into our lungs. Exhaust pollution is worst in cities that have a lot of traffic and where the climate is often sunny and mild such as Los Angeles, California. In these conditions the sunshine triggers chemical reactions, creating a murky brown layer known as photochemical smog. The smog is poisonous to plants, and it irritates people's eyes and lungs. It can be reduced by making cars burn gas more cleanly, but with so many cars on the roads, it is difficult to bring under control.

▶ This color-coded satellite map shows the ozone hole as a jagged, dark blue ring above Antarctica. On New Zealand's South Island and near the tip of South America the thin ozone layer makes it easy to get sunburned, even on cloudy days.

The ozone hole

Ozone is one of the worst ingredients of photochemical smog because it attacks living cells. But much higher up in the atmosphere a layer of natural ozone protects us against harmful radiation from the Sun. This vital shield, between 12–28 mi. (25–45km) high, has been in place for millions of years. But in the early 1980s scientists discovered that the layer seemed to thin and then disappear over Antarctica during the southern winter. Several years later thinning was found over the North Pole too.

We depend on the ozone layer, so this discovery was extremely serious news. Remarkably, it had been predicted more than ten years earlier by two American scientists, Mario Molina and Sherwood Rowland. They found that high-level ozone could be destroyed by chemicals called chlorofluorocarbons, or CFCs. At the time CFCs were widely used in aerosols, refrigerators, and plastics, and large amounts escaped into the air. Once airborne, CFCs drift up into the ozone layer. There they break down ozone molecules, and they keep doing this for many years. The world's reaction to this crisis was unusually fast and effective (see page 48). Today the ozone hole is still with us, but it shows signs of healing. Impressively, by 2040 it may have finally closed.

▼ Smoke from power plants and heavy industries contains sulfur dioxide, the main cause of acid rain. In the air this gas forms tiny droplets of sulfuric acid—the same substance found in car batteries.

The greenhouse effect

If you get into a car that has been parked in the sunshine, the temperature inside is often much higher than it is outside. This is only one example of the greenhouse effect, something that is essential for life on Earth. The greenhouse effect keeps our planet warm—without it, most of the surface would be frozen solid. In recent years air pollution has increased the greenhouse effect, making Earth's temperature rise. If it continues, this worldwide change could be the biggest one ever caused by human beings.

▲ Heated by sunshine, mist rises over a lake and vaporizes into the air. Water vapor is the most important greenhouse gas. If the world continues to warm up, there could be a lot more of it in the air—something that would make Earth even warmer.

▼ The atmosphere is like an insulating jacket wrapped around Earth. Because it traps heat, it warms the planet's surface by more than 86°F (30°C). Without it, life would only be possible in the tropics, and most of the world's water would be frozen solid.

How the greenhouse effect works

When sunlight reaches Earth, some of it is reflected back into space, but most of it travels through the atmosphere until it hits the planet's surface. There it warms up the land and the oceans, making Earth give off energy in return. This outgoing energy is different from sunlight. It has a long wavelength, which makes it invisible, and it is given off from all of Earth's surface 24 hours every day. Unlike sunlight, this energy can be absorbed by some of the gases that are found in air. This difference is crucial because it means that outgoing energy finds it more difficult to escape into space. As a result, Earth clings onto its heat, staying warmer than it would be otherwise.

▶ These two diagrams show how the greenhouse effect works and what happens when extra greenhouse gases build up in the air. With a stable greenhouse gas layer (diagram A), the planet collects heat from sunshine, but at the same time it loses energy through long-wave radiation that travels into space. If greenhouse gases increase (diagram B), this balance changes. Less long-wave radiation escapes, so the planet keeps gaining energy. As a result, it warms up.

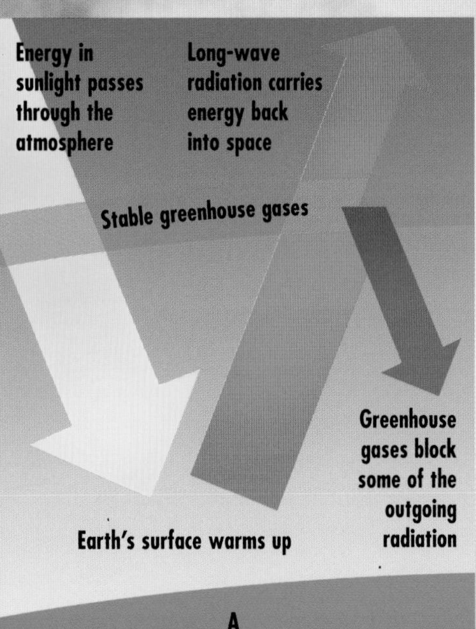

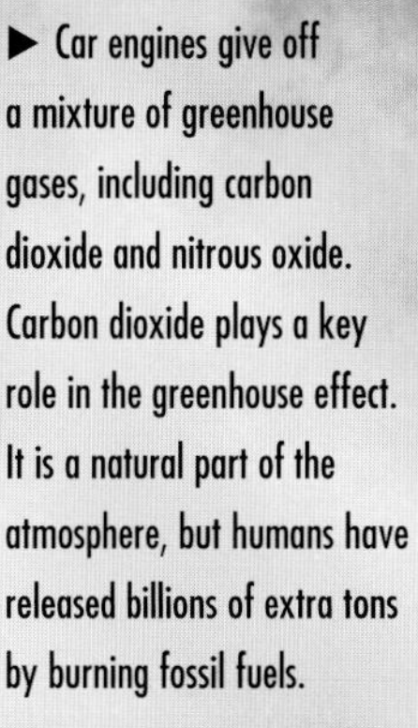

▶ Car engines give off a mixture of greenhouse gases, including carbon dioxide and nitrous oxide. Carbon dioxide plays a key role in the greenhouse effect. It is a natural part of the atmosphere, but humans have released billions of extra tons by burning fossil fuels.

◀ Humans have created some greenhouse gases—such as CFCs, or chlorofluorocarbons—that did not exist on Earth before. Until the 1980s CFCs were used as coolants in refrigerators. These powerful greenhouse gases were phased out after the discovery of the ozone hole, and levels in the atmosphere have recently started to fall.

Greenhouse gases

Our closest neighbor, the Moon, does not have an atmosphere, and its nighttime temperature can plunge to –274°F (–170°C). But back on Earth the atmosphere and its greenhouse gases keep conditions favorable for life. Water vapor accounts for around two thirds of the greenhouse effect. The remaining one third is produced by carbon dioxide, methane, nitrous oxide, and man-made gases (see page 37). Since 1750 humans have increased the carbon dioxide level by almost one third because carbon dioxide is given off when fossil fuels are burned. We have also increased the levels of all the other greenhouse gases.

A changing balance

With greenhouse gas levels rising, the greenhouse effect is increasing too. Most scientists believe that this is why Earth's surface is warming up—a disturbing development that you can read about on the next page. So far global warming has been minimal, but two uncomfortable facts mean that we face a greater danger in the future. Firstly, most greenhouse gases are an inevitable side effect of the way we live. If we want to reduce them, we will have to change our lifestyles. Secondly, some greenhouse gases are very long-lived. Even if we stop releasing them now, they will remain overhead for years to come.

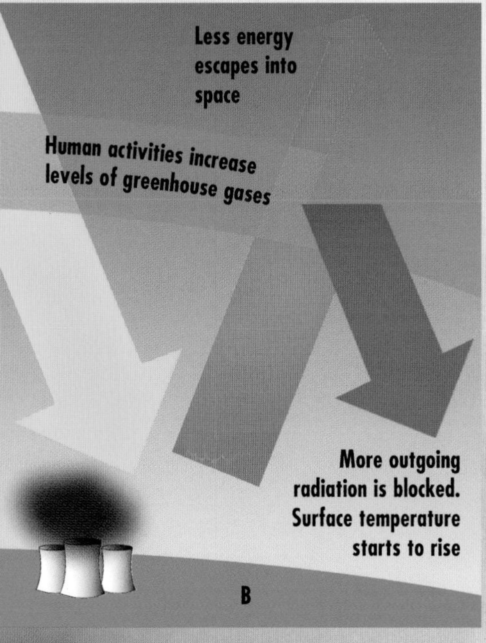

▶ Rice terraces, seen here on the Indonesian island of Bali, are a source of methane—a powerful greenhouse gas. Methane is released whenever anything rots in stagnant water, and it is also given off by grazing mammals. During the last 250 years the atmosphere's methane level has doubled. The construction of reservoirs and the growth of farming are mostly to blame.

Climate change

In 2003 forest fires burned throughout Europe as the continent experienced its warmest summer on record. In 1998 the entire world recorded its warmest year for at least 100 years—possibly for more than 1,000 years. Figures like these showcase a disturbing trend—one that has almost certainly been triggered by the human race. By polluting the atmosphere, we have strengthened the greenhouse effect, and rising temperatures are the result. In the coming years climate change will have far-reaching effects—for us, for our food supply, and for all of the natural world.

▲ In southern Europe a pine forest is swallowed up during the fires of 2003. As the world warms up, disasters like this are likely to happen more often, threatening houses, people, and wildlife.

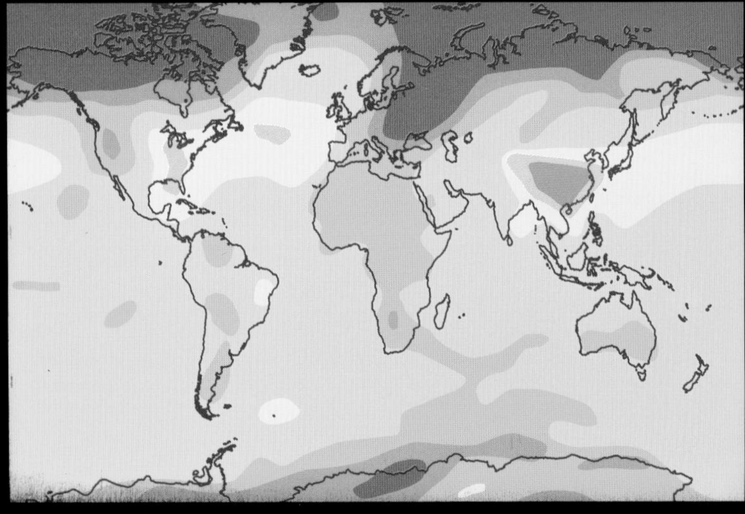

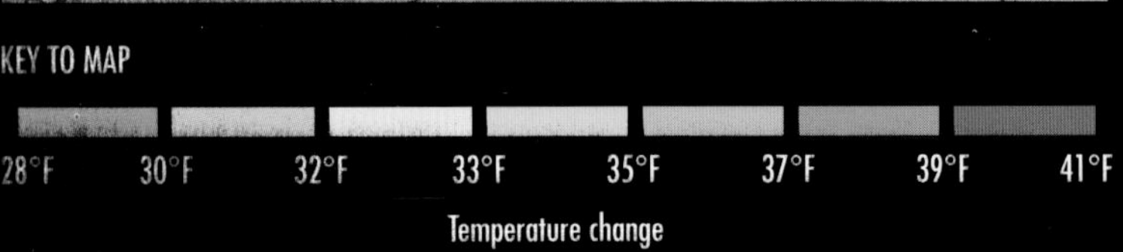

▲ According to IPCC predictions, the world's average surface temperature could rise by up to 41°F (5°C) over the course of the next 100 years. This map shows the temperature change expected by 2050 during the winter months in the Northern Hemisphere.

Patterns in the past

Climate change is almost as old as Earth itself. In the past ice ages have plunged the planet into a long-lasting freeze, while periods called interglacials have brought much warmer conditions—the last one started around 10,000 years ago and is continuing today. Up to a point, warm conditions are good because they encourage plants to grow. But too much warmth can have very damaging effects, especially if the change is fast. That type of change is exactly what most scientists think we are experiencing today.

Who is to blame?

Natural climate change is caused by many factors, which means that it is impossible to predict. This, in turn, makes it very difficult to decide if human activities are partly to blame. A small minority of scientists believes that today's global warming is just a temporary problem that will soon correct itself. Others think that it is significant, but they do not believe that human activities are the cause. But most experts strongly disagree. According to the Intergovernmental Panel on Climate Change (IPCC), global warming is happening now, and humans are to blame.

◀ In a warmer world crop failures from droughts will be more common.

Cause and effect

If you live in a region that has a cool climate, global warming might sound like a good thing. But a steep rise in Earth's surface temperature could make life difficult in many ways. Some parts of the world will become hotter and drier, including regions that supply much of the world's food. With more heat energy in the atmosphere and in the oceans, other areas could be hit by powerful hurricanes and typhoons. In a warmer world polar ice will melt, and seawater will expand. In the next 100 years this could raise the sea level by more than 3 ft. (1m), flooding low-lying coasts and islands. These changes will be difficult enough for people, but for many plants and animals they could be disastrous.

To reverse global warming, we will have to reduce the amount of greenhouse gases that we release. This is a huge challenge, and as you will find out in Chapter 3, there are many ideas—and disagreements—about how this should be done.

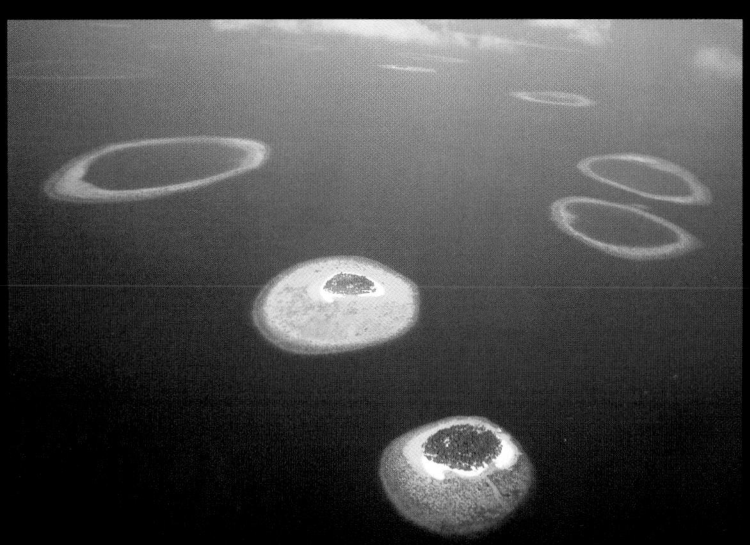

▲ Coral islands are often just a few feet above sea level, putting them in the firing line from global warming. Some island states—such as Tuvalu in the Pacific Ocean—have threatened to sue countries that do not control their output of greenhouse gases.

Wildlife under threat

Because living things evolve, they are able to adapt to gradual changes in the world around them. However, evolution is a slow process—much too slow for animals and plants to keep up with today's rapidly changing world. As a result, a record number of species are finding it very difficult to survive.

Changing times

One hundred years ago most people believed that wildlife existed to be exploited, whatever and wherever it was. Animals were hunted without any thought for conservation, and some species were pushed to the edge of extinction. In 1911 George V—the British king—took part in a hunt in India that killed 39 tigers in only 11 days. Fortunately, attitudes have changed, and fewer people support this type of careless killing. But despite this, thousands of species are already on the endangered list—simply because they share the planet with us.

◀ The bittern—a type of heron that lives in reeds—is a typical casualty of the changing world. Hundreds of years ago it was hunted for food, but today it is more threatened by the disappearance of its natural habitat.

▼ The fight to save the tiger is one of the major conservation challenges. Tigers are under threat from habitat destruction and the illegal trade in their body parts, which are used in oriental medicines.

Deadly competitors

Some of the worst accidental damage to wildlife has been caused by animals and plants that humans have spread around the world. This may sound harmless, but in isolated places introduced species can drive native ones into extinction. For example, New Zealand's birds have been decimated by European mammals, while Hawaii's wildlife has been swamped by animals and plants from five continents. The result is that a limited number of successful species now appear all over the world.

As well as introduced species, wild plants and animals have to deal with human beings. As our population grows, natural habitats shrink, leaving less room for the natural world. Small animals can often survive on small areas of land, but for larger ones, from tigers to giant pandas, shortage of living space can be a deadly threat.

▲ Over collection and habitat destruction threaten many of the world's flowering plants, especially tropical orchids. More than 5,000 species of flowering plants are listed as being endangered, but the figure is sure to rise as scientists conduct more research.

Wildlife in a warmer world

In recent years conservationists have had some spectacular successes in rescuing endangered species—you can find out about some of them on pages 54–55. But in the 21st century wildlife faces a new menace that will be very difficult to control. This threat is global warming, and unlike hunting or habitat loss, it could affect the majority of species on Earth.

For scientists the warmer world is still new territory, and no one knows how well—or badly—the planet's animals and plants will cope. But some recent projections, published by a panel of scientists in 2004, had alarming results. The team studied six of the world's richest wildlife regions and used computers to predict how more than 1,000 different species would fare. They found that by 2050 between 15 and 37 percent of them would no longer exist.

Winners and losers

With something as complex as climate change, future predictions are often wrong. For example, when global warming was first detected, some scientists predicted a 26 ft. (8m) rise in the sea level by the year 2100. Today most experts think that this figure is a huge overestimate. But even if today's predictions are wrong and animals and plants cope much better than expected, thousands of species are still likely to disappear. Global warming is already under way, and it cannot be stopped in a hurry. For many borderline species human help could mean the difference between survival and extinction.

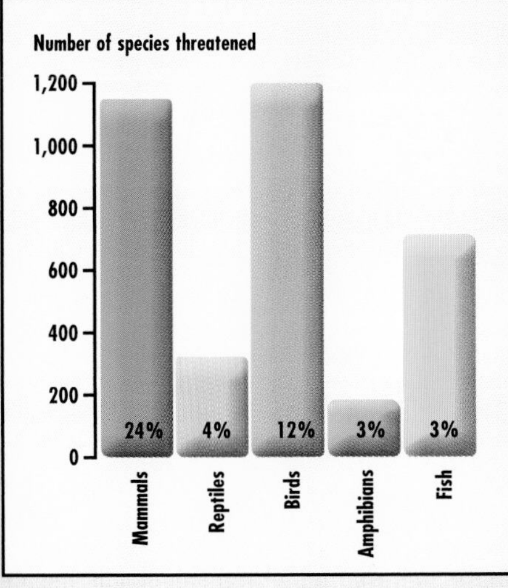

◀ This chart shows the number of vertebrate species that are currently listed as critically endangered, endangered, or vulnerable in the 2002 Red Data Lists. For example, almost 1,200 bird species are threatened—or 12 percent of all bird species on Earth. For fish in particular these figures are only the tip of the iceberg because many species have not yet been given a "health check" by scientists. For more information on Red Data Lists, see page 44.

▼ Polar bears need sea ice to hunt because they attack seals when they come to the surface to breathe. In a warmer world most of the Arctic Ocean could stay ice free all winter, putting pressure on one of the world's largest carnivores.

SUMMARY OF CHAPTER 2: PLANET UNDER PRESSURE

The people planet
This book began by exploring the living world and the connections that keep it working. This chapter looked at something that is disturbing these connections: the ever-growing human race. Today there are more than six billion people on the planet, and the total is quickly rising. Because there are so many of us, we have some type of effect on almost every other species on Earth. Thanks to humans, an increasing number of plants and animals are finding it difficult to survive.

Most fast-food packaging is designed to be used only once before being thrown away.

Disappearing habitats
To stay alive, the human population needs an enormous supply of food. This is the main reason behind the wave of habitat destruction that has affected many parts of the world. Habitats are destroyed to make space for farmland and to provide the raw materials and fuel that we use. They are also cleared to make room for towns, cities, and roads. During the last 50 years habitat clearance has accelerated as more people switch to an urban way of life.

Waste and global warming
Unlike people several generations ago, we live in a consumer age. Our modern lifestyles use a lot of energy, and almost all of it comes from fossil fuels: oil, coal, and natural gas. As consumers, we generate ever-growing amounts of waste—from plastic packaging to the gases released by chimneys and car exhausts. Some of these gases damage the ozone layer, produce acid rain, or trigger photochemical smog. Others are responsible for global warming—a change that will bring major problems for the living world. As the planet's surface warms by up to 41°F (5°C) over the next 100 years, thousands of plant and animal species could become extinct.

Go further . . .

Read the latest headlines at the UN Food and Agriculture Organization, an international agency that helps combat hunger around the world: www.fao.org/english/newsroom

Find out more about climate change and its effects by visiting www.blueplanetbiomes.org/climate.htm

Discover more about endangered species by using the searchable Red List database created by the IUCN: www.redlist.org/search/search-basic.html

Global Warming by Fred Pearce (Dorling Kindersley, 2002)

Agronomist
Studies farming techniques and food production.

Botanist
Studies plants and how they grow.

Climatologist
Examines the way that the climate works and how it changes.

Demographer
Investigates population size and the factors that make it rise or fall.

Hydrologist
Analyzes the world's water resources, on the surface and underground.

Zoologist
Studies animals and how they live.

Learn about the National Wildlife Refuge System at the Smithsonian Museum of Natural History.
Smithsonian Museum of Natural History
10th St. and Constitution Ave. NW
Washington, D.C. 20560
Phone: (202) 357-2700
www.mnh.si.edu

Find out how one of the world's biggest cities has grown over the centuries by visiting the Museum of London.
Museum of London
London Wall
London EC2Y 5HN
England
Phone: +44 (0) 870 444 3852
www.museumoflondon.org.uk

CHAPTER 3

Sustainable world

Imagine that Earth is a business. Its future prospects do not look great. Every year its production lines work faster and faster, but its raw materials are dwindling at a frightening rate. In the drive to boost output, maintenance is often ignored, and the company's power and water supplies are under strain. This is a dangerous combination, and without urgent action the business looks bound to fail.

Farfetched? Possibly. But in many ways this is the world we live in today. For too long people have treated the world any way they want, without worrying about the effects. But as we have seen in Chapter 2, the past is catching up with us, and it is clear that things will have to change. In this chapter you can read about what is being done to reduce our impact so that planet Earth can be nursed back to health.

Ecofriendly, energy-efficient housing near Croydon in southern England

▲ Whaling is a classic example of the misuse of the planet's resources, with several species being hunted to the brink of extinction. At present commercial whaling is suspended, but some countries are eager for it to restart.

Conserving resources

Humans do not have a good track record at using the world's resources. Too often, we use them up in an uncontrolled rush as everyone scrambles for a share. The result is environmental damage—sometimes on an enormous scale. Fortunately, there are signs that the world is moving away from this "grab-it-while-you-can" lifestyle.

Sustainable use

Many resources can be used only once because they take so long to form. Oil is one example; another is the "fossil" groundwater that is used to irrigate fields. Once these run out, it could take hundreds or even millions of human lifetimes for them to be replaced. But some resources are renewed all the time. These include living things and energy from the Sun and also everything that the Sun powers such as the wind and waves. Because the Sun keeps delivering fresh supplies of energy, these resources can be harvested year after year. To create a sustainable world, we need to depend much more on resources like these. At the same time we must limit the harvesting of animals and plants so that nature has time to replace what we use.

Action for change

One hundred years ago loggers were cutting down North America's giant redwoods trees, and whales were being hunted in their thousands. But, slowly, people began to realize that these resources could disappear forever. In 1946 whaling was regulated for the first time, and later, in the 1970s, environmental groups, such as Greenpeace and Friends of the Earth, were born. Their early campaigns marked the start of the modern environmental age.

▼ For most of the year this house generates all the energy that it needs, using technology that is available today. It is powered by sunlight—the ultimate renewable resource. Where possible, the house is built using local materials, helping reduce the amount of pollution caused by construction and transportation.

Photovoltaic cells on the roof turn sunlight directly into electricity, powering all of the domestic appliances.

A small wind turbine provides back-up power in cloudy weather.

Insulated wooden walls help keep the house warm in the winter and cool in the summer. The insulation is made from recycled materials, helping reduce construction costs and waste.

Renewable resources at home

In a sustainable world changes would begin at home. The house shown on these two pages is designed with sustainable living in mind. It is well insulated in order to keep it warm in the winter, and most of the energy it needs is provided by solar collectors and photovoltaic cells (see pages 50–51). In sunny conditions a house like this would make surplus electricity, which would be fed to local electric companies. Cutting down on waste is also an important part of "green" living. In this house food waste is used to make garden compost, while paper, metals, and plastics are sorted so they can be recycled. For more details about recycling, see pages 52–53.

A shared responsibility

If all new homes were like this, it would really help conserve the world's resources. On a personal level you can help by the choices you make—because "green" consumers encourage businesses to change. But no matter how careful you are, you will not be able to stop all of the environmental problems that affect the world today. Some are just much too big. That is why many "green" groups want governments to make tougher laws. They believe that businesses should share in the global cleanup by taking responsibility for environmental problems that they cause.

Tiny microprocessors positioned throughout the house are linked to a central computer. They automatically adjust lighting and heating levels by sensing conditions both inside and outside.

A rain-collecting system provides enough water for bathing, dishwashing, flushing, and laundry. Wastewater from the kitchen and shower is used to irrigate the garden, instead of being disposed of with sewage.

Under-floor heating, using piped water from the main tank, distributes warmth evenly throughout the house.

▶ Direct action has helped put environmental issues in the headlines. Here, Greenpeace volunteers are protesting about air pollution from the top of an incinerator chimney.

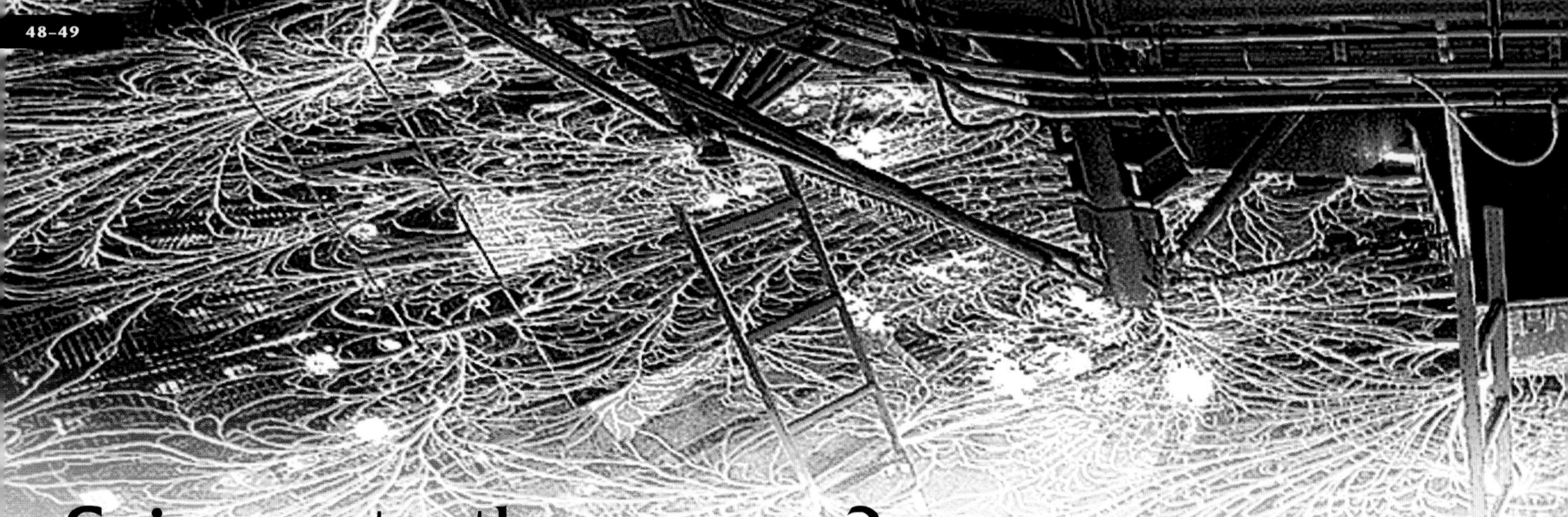

Science to the rescue?

During the last 50 years technology has revolutionized the way we live. Could it also help overcome some of the environmental problems that we face? Many scientists think so. But technology has its limits—sometimes the best way to fix a problem is not to make things more complicated but instead to make them simpler and more safe.

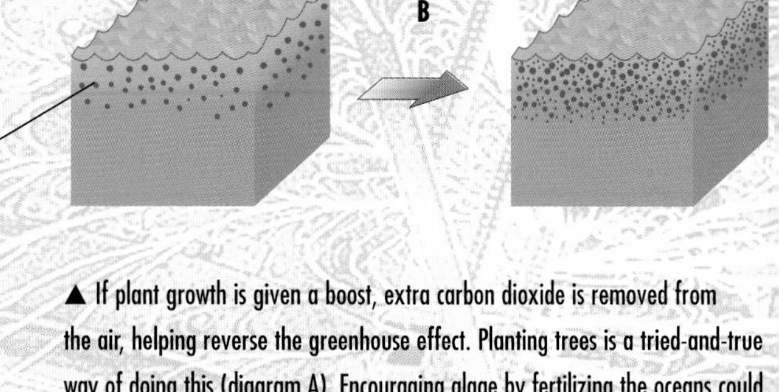

▲ If plant growth is given a boost, extra carbon dioxide is removed from the air, helping reverse the greenhouse effect. Planting trees is a tried-and-true way of doing this (diagram A). Encouraging algae by fertilizing the oceans could also help (diagram B), but it might have unwanted side effects on marine life.

Closing the ozone hole

When scientists discovered the ozone hole in the 1980s, they realized that rapid action was needed to repair it. The hole was caused mostly by CFCs (see page 37), so it was vital that these chemicals were phased out. It seemed to be an almost impossible task, but effective substitutes for CFCs were found, and an international agreement—the Montreal Protocol—was created to set a timetable for the change. Because of this agreement and new technology, a major environmental crisis was successfully averted.

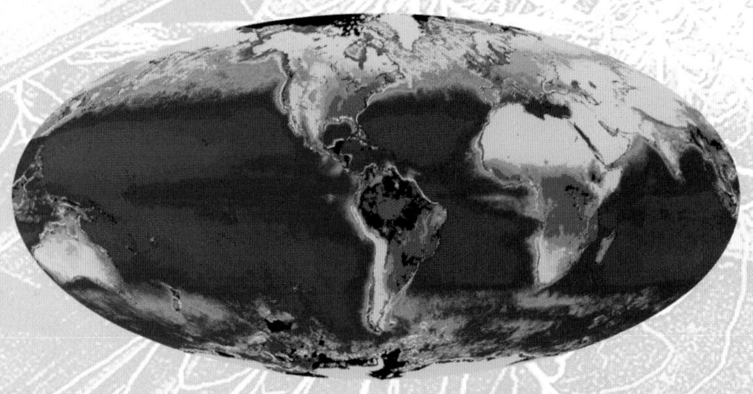

▲ This false-color satellite image shows the density of microscopic algae—which absorb carbon dioxide—in the world's oceans. Red areas have the most algae, while light blue have the least.

Fighting global warming

Global warming presents an even bigger challenge than the ozone hole because it affects important aspects of modern life. Somehow we have to reduce the atmosphere's carbon dioxide level, and it is possible that new technology could help. One high-tech solution, first suggested in the 1990s, involves "fertilizing" the oceans with iron to boost the growth of algae, which absorb carbon dioxide from the air. Another involves storing carbon dioxide by pumping it into the ground. These ideas look good on paper, and energy companies like them because they mean we could continue to burn fossil fuels. But many experts doubt that they would really work on a global scale. A much simpler way of locking up carbon is to plant new forests. Even better, we could tackle the source of the problem by using renewable energy, which produces no carbon dioxide at all.

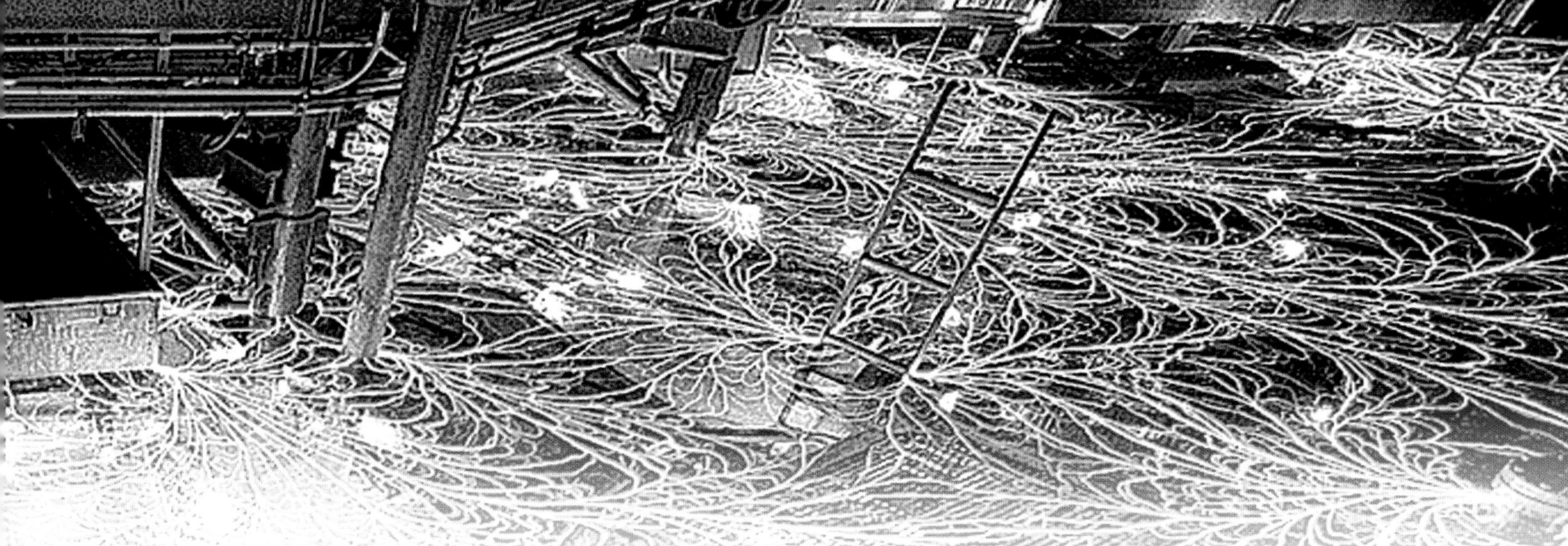

▲ Electricity flashes around the Z Machine, an experimental device used in nuclear fusion research. The machine can heat gases to a temperature of around 18,000,000°F (10,000,000°C)—almost hot enough to trigger nuclear fusion, which would release enormous amounts of power.

◀ A research scientist checks a field of genetically modified wheat. GM technology allows scientists to move useful genes between different species—something that traditional breeding techniques cannot do.

The ultimate energy source

In the world of high-tech science the quest to harness nuclear fusion is one of the most ambitious projects of all. Nuclear fusion makes the Sun shine, so it is a process that keeps all of us alive. Unlike nuclear fission, which involves splitting atoms, fusion forces them together. As the atoms fuse, they give off a colossal amount of energy, but they produce no carbon dioxide and very little dangerous waste. Some physicists believe that fusion could be the ultimate answer to the world's energy needs. However, building a fusion reactor is a very difficult task. Despite years of research, fusion power has still not gotten off the ground.

▶ In the developing world new technology can improve daily life without needing a lot of technical know-how or expensive equipment. This Bolivian woman is using a solar stove, which can cut a family's fuel use by 50 percent. Other examples of "appropriate" technology include solar-powered water pumps, pollution-free toilets, and even windup radios.

Farming and food

So far the world's countries have been unable to agree on a global warming action plan. They also disagree about new ways of growing food. One argument is about the use of chemicals—organic farmers try to avoid them altogether because they can damage the environment and end up in human food. Another dispute concerns genetic modification (GM)—a new technology that can create special varieties of animals and plants. As the human population continues to grow, some scientists think that GM technology could be the answer to the world's food problems. Others are firmly opposed to it because modified varieties could contaminate and damage wild species. At the present time the arguments have reached a deadlock. GM crops are widely grown in North America, but they are tightly controlled or even banned in some countries.

Renewable energy

Today almost all of the energy we use comes from fossil fuels or nuclear power. But in the future we will depend much more on renewable sources such as sunlight, wind, and water. Renewable energy is not free, and sometimes it is not as "green" as it seems. But unlike other sources of energy, it is constantly replaced, so it can be harvested forever without running out.

▶ When it is finished, the Three Gorges dam on China's Yangtze (Chang) river will be one of the biggest in the world. As well as generating electricity, it will stop the Yangtze's notorious floods, which have claimed countless lives.

Solar power

Sunlight is by far the biggest source of renewable energy. It is safe and nonpolluting, and in theory it could meet all of our energy needs. Unfortunately, sunlight is not easy to harvest on a large scale, which is why solar power plants are rare. On a local scale using solar energy is much more practical. It can be gathered by solar collectors, which heat water, and by photovoltaic cells, which convert sunlight into electricity. Photovoltaic cells are especially useful because they can be installed almost anywhere—from roofs to the tops of utility poles. In decades to come solar power looks likely to expand in a major way as the price of photovoltaic cells comes down and their efficiency goes up.

▲ The Solar One power plant, near Barstow, California, collects sunlight with 1,800 steerable, computer-controlled mirrors. The sunlight is used to make steam, and this powers a turbine that generates enough electricity for 5,000 homes.

Hydropower

Compared to other renewable energy sources, hydroelectric power already makes a big impact. Gigantic dams spread across the world's largest rivers, generating electricity for millions of factories and homes. A dam can produce pollution-free power for decades, and it can also help supply drinking water and prevent floods and droughts. However, big dams cost a huge amount of money to build, and their reservoirs often flood natural habitats, farmland, and homes. Hydropow[er] will remain important in the future, but tomorrow's dams are likely to be smaller than those being built today.

Wind and waves

Hundreds of years ago windmills were common in some countries. Today their place has been taken by wind turbines, which generate electricity with slender rotating blades. Wind power is not cheap, but it has one key advantage: the wind is often strongest in the winter, when electric power is most needed. But the wind is unreliable, and sometimes it does not blow at all. Many engineers think that wave power has a brighter future because waves contain much more energy. However, wave turbines are still in their experimental phase.

▶ These two students in Benin are maintaining a biogas digester—a simple device that produces methane gas from plant and animal waste. The gas is stored in tanks and is used for cooking and lighting. Biogas systems are cheap to install and easy to run, making them ideal for people who live in rural areas.

◀ "Green" campaigners have divided views about wind turbines. Some are enthusiastic about them, but others feel that they spoil landscapes and harm wildlife without generating much energy in return.

The hydrogen world

Renewable energy has one big drawback: unlike oil, it cannot be carried around. If we are really going to cut back on fossil fuels, a substitute for oil has to be found. That substitute will almost certainly be liquid hydrogen—a pressurized gas that is already being used to power some buses and cars. Hydrogen can be made from water, and it produces no pollution at all when it burns. To make it, electrical energy is needed, and that is where renewable sources play a part. In tomorrow's "hydrogen world" sunshine could be used to make this ideal fuel. As oil is slowly phased out, the days of smoking exhausts and polluted air would become a distant memory.

▶ At this experimental gas station in Germany a car fills up with liquid hydrogen instead of gasoline. On a full tank it can travel 186 mi. (300km). The hydrogen gas is produced by a bank of photovoltaic cells, and it is pressurized to turn it into a liquid.

Reuse and recycling

▼ This futuristic composting plant is in the Environmental Technology Park—an ecofriendly waste processing center on the Mediterranean island of Mallorca. Because space for landfills is short on Mallorca, recycling is a top priority.

What is the difference between a bottle made out of brand-new glass and one made from glass that has been recycled? The answer is very little, except for the impact that they have on the environment. Recycling saves raw materials, and it cuts down on waste and pollution. Reusing objects helps the environment even more. Today recycling is still not foolproof—and too much is thrown away—but in tomorrow's world it will play an increasing part in reducing household waste.

A recycling lineup

Glass and metals are perfect for recycling because they can be melted down and reused almost indefinitely. Paper is not as good because its fibers gradually weaken each time it is used. As a result, it can be recycled only around six or seven times. But even that is a huge saving for the environment, so recycling paper makes a lot of sense. Plastics are much more problematic because there are so many different types. Very few can be melted down and made into the same thing again and again. Instead many plastics are recycled only once by being made into objects such as shopping bags or drainage pipes. After that they are usually thrown away. For a world drowning in waste it is a problem that must be solved.

▶ Color-coded recycling cans are already a common sight, and they are set to become even more widespread. In the future many plastics will go into the same can as kitchen waste because they will be biodegradable.

◀ These wine bottles contain more than 50 percent recycled glass. New glass takes a lot of energy to make, so adding recycled glass reduces the pollution caused by burning fossil fuels.

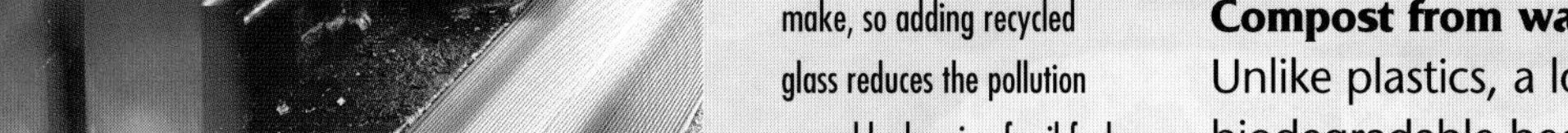

Plastics that rot away

One way of reducing plastic waste is to cut down on packaging that nobody needs, and some countries have introduced charges for throwaway plastic bags. Even better, scientists are trying to devise new types of biodegradable plastics that rot down harmlessly when they are thrown away. Normal plastics are made from oil, but biodegradable plastics are usually made from plant-based products such as cornstarch or cellulose. The challenge is to turn these substances into plastics that are as strong as the ones we use today. Scientists have not done this yet, but the race is on. Success will be well worth the effort because the market for these plastics could be worth $25 billion per year.

Compost from waste

Unlike plastics, a lot of household waste is already biodegradable because nature made it that way. Food and garden waste can all be turned into compost, a natural fertilizer that is spread on fields. At the present time only a small amount of household waste ends up being composted, but with landfill sites overflowing, that is likely to change. To make this type of recycling feasible, waste has to be presorted. Many of us already do this, but local authorities will need to encourage people who do not seem to have the time. One possibility might be to charge people according to how much unrecyclable garbage they throw away. When that happens, being wasteful will not just be shortsighted—it will be expensive too.

▲ Disposable utensils (background image) can be made from recycled plastic, but after being used they are normally thrown away. This is an example of "open-loop" recycling. In "closed-loop" recycling a raw material—such as glass—can be recycled an unlimited number of times.

▼ This bale contains shredded wastepaper, ready to be recycled. At one time old newspapers were useless waste, but due to recycling, they have become a useful commodity.

Wildlife protection

Around the world thousands of different organizations are working hard to protect animals and plants that are under threat. There have been some great successes, with endangered species pulled back from the brink of extinction. Some of these success stories could soon be off the danger list altogether. But protecting wildlife involves some difficult questions. What is the best way to help threatened species? And how can we leave space for wildlife when so many people are short of space themselves?

▲ Costa Rica is one of the world leaders in conservation. More than one fourth of this Central American country is protected by wildlife reserves such as the Rincón de la Vieja national park (above).

Species or habitats?

Many wildlife campaigns focus on individual species such as giant pandas, orangutans, or whales. Without this work, some of these animals might now be extinct in the wild. But with so many species in danger, we cannot afford a separate program for each one. Instead conservationists now give top priority to saving complete habitats so that all the species can take care of themselves. Some reserves are truly vast. One of the largest, Canada's Wood Buffalo National Park, covers 17,550 sq. mi. (45,000km²)—an area as big as Switzerland.

Stopping the wildlife trade

Saving wildlife means tough action against people who exploit endangered species. More than 160 countries have signed the Convention on International Trade in Endangered Species (CITES), which bans the cross-border trade in more than 2,500 animal species and almost ten times as many plants. In ports and airports worldwide customs officials keep on the lookout for species on the CITES lists, as well as for their body parts such as fur, ivory, shells, and bones. Soon DNA testing could help them identify listed species.

Controlling introduced species

Conservation sometimes involves undoing past mistakes. In some countries a huge effort is made to control introduced species that harm native wildlife. In South Africa the worst invaders are trees and shrubs, which have to be cut down and burned. In Australia the main offenders are predators such as foxes. They are trapped or killed with a poison that is harmless to native animals. This is controversial, but scientists are convinced it will help Australia's rarest animals survive.

◀ In 1989 a pile of confiscated tusks was publicly burned in Kenya in order to publicize the fight against the illegal elephant ivory trade. Ivory obtains a high price on the black market—this pile had a street value of around $750,000.

Emergency action

When a species is in really dire straits, drastic measures may be needed to save it. Captive breeding has proved successful with some critically endangered mammals and birds such as the California condor. In 1987 there were only 27 left in zoos, with none in the wild. But by 2004 the population had risen to 215, and around 80 birds had been released from captivity. Sometimes endangered animals are moved to safer homes. The tuatara—a rare lizard from New Zealand—was airlifted from the mainland to several offshore islands, where it does not have to face predatory mammals. With endangered plants, seeds can be stored in special seed banks, where they stay alive for years. This biological "insurance" makes sure that the species lives on.

▲ Using a puppet, a zookeeper feeds a California condor chick at San Diego Zoo in California. The young birds are kept away from people so that they will be able to fend for themselves in the wild.

Paying for wildlife

To survive in the long term, wildlife needs to be wild. But in our overcrowded world people need space too. Somehow we have to find a way of living with wildlife, instead of pushing it aside. One possible solution is to charge a fee to view wildlife. The national parks of Costa Rica have become an important economic asset because they attract many foreign visitors. In southern Africa tourists flock to see elephants and rhinoceroses, while all over the world, from North America to Australia, people pay for the unbeatable excitement of whale watching. Tourism cannot protect all of the world's wildlife—and it can cause environmental problems of its own. But if it is carefully managed, tourism could help preserve rare species in tomorrow's world.

▲ In South Africa a shrub-clearance team hacks away at invading plants that are smothering native vegetation. The entrance fees charged by national parks help fund this important work.

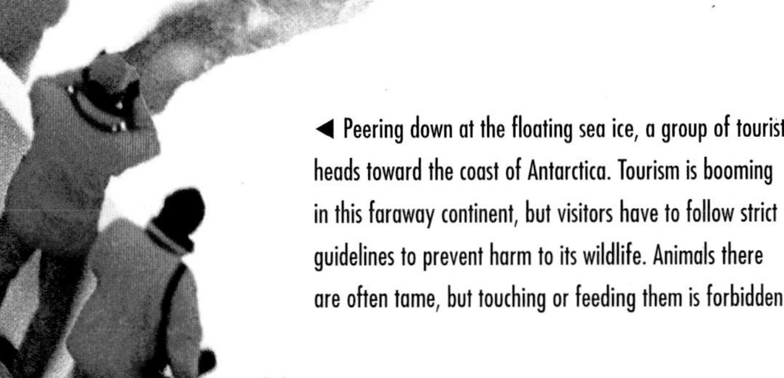

◀ Peering down at the floating sea ice, a group of tourists heads toward the coast of Antarctica. Tourism is booming in this faraway continent, but visitors have to follow strict guidelines to prevent harm to its wildlife. Animals there are often tame, but touching or feeding them is forbidden.

The future

By the year 2100 the world's population may have stopped growing, but there could be twice as many people as there are now. With so many humans needing food and somewhere to live, the pressure on our planet will be intense. So what will planet Earth be like? Will it be more polluted, with species disappearing at an ever-faster rate? Or will it be on the road to recovery, after all the mistakes of the past? Although 2100 is a long time away, the future depends on decisions that are being made today.

Global cooperation

In 2004 more than 120 countries signed an ambitious agreement that aims to save endangered species and their habitats. Within six years each country is expected to have at least ten percent of its land under protection, and by 2012 ocean life will also be included. If all goes to plan, the outlook will be much better for the world's wildlife. In other areas talks are under way to control all types of environmental problems—from packaging waste to pollution at sea. This truly international effort is a promising sign for the planet's future.

Business as usual

Unfortunately, agreeing to do something is not the same as doing it. Environmental agreements can be hard to enforce, and they cost money. Whenever there is a choice between big business and the environment, business often seems to win. Tropical rain forests highlight this dilemma—despite being some of the world's richest wildlife habitats, they are disappearing fast as loggers, farmers, and miners move in. In the fight to preserve them local conservationists literally risk their lives.

▶ Without action to save the environment, Earth's future looks bleak. The next 100 years could bring a collapse in the world's biological diversity, as habitats become fragmented and global warming takes its toll. In this type of world the lucky minority would live in comfort, but a range of environmental problems—from water pollution to soil erosion—would make life extremely difficult for most people. Today this global split has already begun.

Piling on the pressure

During the next 100 years the natural world will be under pressure in other ways. In rapidly developing countries, such as China and India, millions of newly prosperous people will become Western-style consumers. They will expect the same services and products that Westerners enjoy such as air travel, fast cars, and fast food. By 2100 global food production will have to double—an enormous challenge that could have serious side effects for other living things. As well as being efficient, agriculture will have to be much more reliable—if not, billions of the world's poorest people could face famines that are much worse than the ones that occur today.

Differing opinions

Some experts think that rising prosperity is the key to solving the planet's problems. If they are right, in 2100 Earth will be busier, more built up, but less polluted than it is today. In this future world human ingenuity would help protect wildlife, and problems like global warming would be under control. But many environmentalists are not convinced by this picture. Without strong action, they believe that most of the world's tropical rain forests could vanish in the next 50 years, followed by other threatened habitats such as wetlands and coral reefs. By 2100 some people could be more prosperous, but the world as a whole could be a much poorer place.

An ecological future

The future is notoriously difficult to predict, and even the experts can be wrong. In the 1960s, for example, some scientists predicted a population catastrophe by the year 2000, with people struggling to survive on an overloaded planet. Others thought that by 2000 people would be living permanently on the Moon. Both predictions turned out to be wrong, and so will many of the predictions that are made today. As we look forward into the future, however, there are two pieces of genuinely good news. The first is that nature is extremely resilient and can bounce back if it is given a chance. The second is that millions of people now care passionately about the environment. In a world affected by many problems that is the most promising sign of all.

◀ If humans manage to master the art of sustainable living, tomorrow's world could be less polluted than today's—despite a huge increase in the global population. In this type of world energy would come almost entirely from renewable resources, and all everyday products, from cars to computers, would be designed to be recycled once their useful life is over. The world's surviving wilderness areas would be fully protected from exploitation, just like Antarctica is today.

SUMMARY OF CHAPTER 3: SUSTAINABLE WORLD

Sustainable living

For most of human history people have been bad at conserving the world's resources—and even worse at preventing pollution and waste. This has created a range of environmental problems, which were explored in Chapter 2. This chapter looked at possible solutions to these problems involving changes in the way people live. The goal of these changes is sustainability. In other words, they focus on resources that can be renewed or recycled, instead of ones that are used once and then thrown away.

As solar power technology improves, sunlight will meet more of our energy needs in the future.

Scientific solutions

In the search for sustainability science has an important role to play. Improvements in technology mean that it is becoming easier and cheaper to harness energy from renewable sources such as sunlight, wind, or water. In the future hydrogen technology could make driving almost pollution free, and biodegradable plastics and improved recycling facilities could reduce the problem of waste. But technology will not provide all the answers. Without careful testing, some scientific advances—such as the genetic modification of crops and livestock—could make environmental problems worse.

Making the change

In the 21st century the human population could almost double before it finally levels out. At the same time global warming will become more noticeable, creating problems for the living world. These changes are already under way, so we cannot escape their effects. But concern about the environment is beginning to spur people and governments into action. If humans make the shift to a sustainable way of life—in which species and habitats are protected and resources are conserved—our planet could be on the road to recovery.

Go further . . .

Visit the UN Environment Program's youth site—a great place to find out what young people are doing to protect the planet: www.unep.org/Documents/Default.asp?DocumentID=295

For the latest news about Friends of the Earth's environmental campaigns, visit its Web site: www.foe.org

The Greenpeace International Web site is full of information about environmental issues and direct action taken by Greenpeace volunteers: www.greenpeace.org/international_en

Environmental campaigner
Raises awareness about environmental problems, sometimes by direct action.

Environmental consultant
Advises companies about environmental problems and ways to avoid them.

Forest ranger
Conserves wildlife by working in national parks and forests.

Futurologist
Predicts the future by analyzing current trends.

Geneticist
Studies genes, DNA, and inheritance.

See wildlife in action by visiting San Diego Zoo, including The Center for the Reproduction of Endangered Species (CRES).
San Diego Zoo
2920 Zoo Drive
San Diego, CA 92101
Phone: (619) 231-1515
www.sandiegozoo.org

Contact the Center for Alternative Technology—Europe's leading ecocenter—to see demonstrations of all types of environment-friendly inventions.
Center for Alternative Technology
Machynlleth, Powys SY20 9AZ
Wales
Phone: +44 (0)1654 705950
www.cat.org.uk

Glossary

acid rain
Rain that has been made acidic by pollutants in the air.

adaptation
In living things any feature that has been produced by evolution. Adaptations help living things survive and reproduce.

alga (plural: algae)
Simple, plantlike organisms that grow by collecting the energy in sunlight. Most algae live in water.

"appropriate" technology
Technology that uses local resources and skills, instead of those that are brought in from other parts of the world.

aquifer
A natural reservoir of underground water. The water is usually held in small pores and cracks in rocks.

atmosphere
The blanket of gases that surrounds Earth. The atmosphere is composed mostly of nitrogen and oxygen, with small amounts of other gases such as water vapor and carbon dioxide.

atom
The smallest particle of an element, such as carbon, from which all matter is made.

bacterium (plural: bacteria)
A microbe with a single cell. Bacteria are the smallest, simplest, and most ancient living things on Earth.

biodegradable
A word that describes anything that can be broken down and digested by living things.

biodiversity
The number of different species in a given area or on the planet as a whole.

biome
A characteristic community of plants and animals such as grassland, desert, or tropical rain forest.

biosphere
All the parts of the world where living things are found.

broad-leaved tree
A tree that usually has broad, flat leaves such as an oak, beech, or eucalyptus. Unlike conifers, broad-leaved trees are flowering plants.

bromeliad
A type of plant with stiff, spiky leaves that often grows on tree trunks and branches.

canopy
The upper layer of a forest, formed by the interlocking branches of neighboring trees.

carbon
A chemical element found in all living things. Carbon forms thousands of different compounds in nature. Thousands more—including plastics, solvents, and medicines—have been artificially made by chemists.

carbon dioxide
A colorless, carbon-containing gas. It is taken in by plants when they carry out photosynthesis and given out by animals when they release energy from food.

cellulose
A carbon-containing substance that plants make and use as a building material.

CFC
Short for chlorofluorocarbon, CFCs are man-made compounds that can destroy the ozone layer.

compost
A crumbly mixture containing the remains of plants, as well as the microbes that break them down. Compost is good for improving the fertility of soil.

compound
A chemical that contains atoms of several elements combined in a particular way.

conserve
To minimize the use of any natural resource, such as tropical trees or a fossil fuel, so that it does not run out.

Logging in North America

continental drift
The gradual movement of continents across Earth's surface.

decompose
To rot down. In nature decomposition is carried out by bacteria and other microbes, which break down and recycle dead remains.

deforestation
The permanent removal of a forest, often to make way for farmland.

demographic transition
A slowdown in population growth that occurs when a country becomes developed.

developed country
A country with high average incomes and well-developed services such as hospitals and schools. Most developed countries are industrialized.

developing country
A country where average incomes are low and where many people do not have access to basic services such as clean water and education.

endemic species
A species that is found in only one place.

environment
The setting around any living thing. The word "environment" can also be used in a much wider sense to mean the setting for all of the living world.

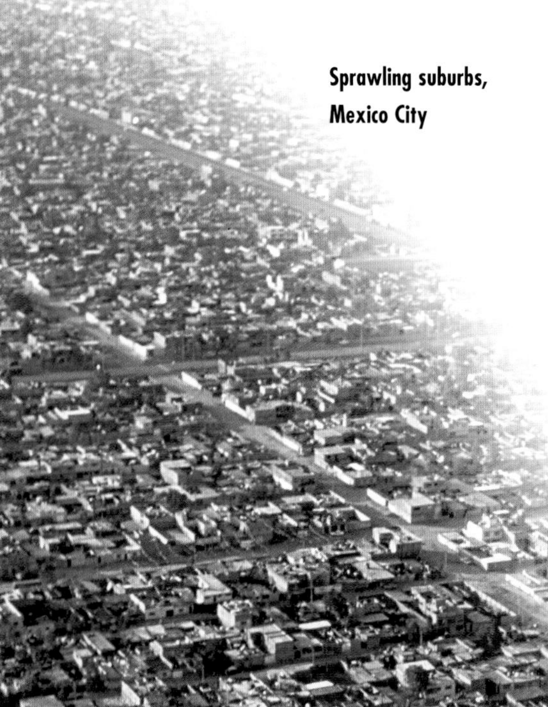

Sprawling suburbs, Mexico City

evolution
A very slow process of change that enables living things to adapt to the world around them. During evolution new species develop, and existing ones eventually become extinct.

extinction
The permanent disappearance of a species.

fossil
The preserved remains of living things. Some fossils are formed by remains, while others are signs of things that living creatures leave behind such as burrows or footprints.

fossil fuels
Fuels formed in sedimentary rocks by the fossilized remains of prehistoric plants that lived millions of years ago. Fossil fuels include oil, coal, and natural gas.

gene
A chemical instruction passed on from parents to their offspring when living things breed. Genes help build living things, and they control the way they work.

genetic modification (GM)
A way of giving a living thing new features by inserting genes from another species.

global warming
A worldwide rise in temperatures caused by the buildup of the greenhouse effect.

"green"
A label used for people or political parties that are committed to helping the natural environment.

greenhouse effect
A feature of the atmosphere that stops heat from escaping into space. The greenhouse effect keeps Earth much warmer than it would normally be.

groundwater
Water that flows through spaces deep underground. See also **aquifer**.

habitat
The surroundings that a particular species needs to survive. Most species live in only one habitat, but some can survive in several.

herbicide
Any chemical that kills plants.

hydroelectric power
Electric power that is generated by moving water. The electricity is produced by turbines at the base of a dam.

hydrological cycle
The natural cycle that replenishes all the freshwater on Earth. It begins when heat from the Sun evaporates seawater and turns it into rain or snow. Also called the water cycle.

industrialized country
A country where most people work in factories and offices and few are farmers.

intensive farming
Farming that produces high crop yields but that depends on a lot of herbicides, fertilizer, and fuel.

introduced species
A species that has been spread by people to a region where it does not naturally occur.

landfill
A site where waste is disposed of by piling it up and then covering it with soil.

methane
A colorless gas that is produced when things rot in swampy ground.

microbe
Any living thing that is too small to be seen with the naked eye such as a bacterium.

mineral
A naturally occurring chemical in Earth's crust. Mixtures of minerals make up rocks.

nitrogen
The most abundant gas in the atmosphere. Nitrogen is an important ingredient in proteins, so it is needed by all living things.

Young giant panda, China

photovoltaic cell
A device that converts the energy in sunlight directly into electricity.

recycling
Reprocessing any product so that its raw materials can be used again.

Red Data Lists
Lists of threatened species, prepared and updated by the International Union for the Conservation of Nature and Natural Resources (IUCN).

reserves
Stocks of fuels or minerals that are known to exist but that have not yet been extracted and used.

species
A single type of living thing. The members of a species can all breed with each other, but they do not normally breed with anything else.

sulfur dioxide
An acid gas that is produced when sulfur-containing fuels, such as coal, are burned.

nitrous oxide
A compound of nitrogen produced when fuels are burned. Along with other nitrogen oxides, it is a major cause of air pollution in places where there is heavy traffic.

nuclear fission
A way of producing energy by splitting atoms of heavy elements such as uranium. Nuclear fission produces waste that remains dangerously radioactive for many years.

nuclear fusion
A method of producing energy by forcing atoms to fuse, or combine.

organic farming
A way of farming that tries to use land in a sustainable way. Organic farmers do not use artificial fertilizers or herbicides.

ozone
A poisonous, colorless gas that contains the same type of atoms as oxygen. High up in the atmosphere, the ozone layer absorbs harmful rays in sunlight.

ozone hole
A gap in the ozone layer caused by man-made chemicals, such as CFCs, that have escaped into the air.

pesticide
Any chemical designed to kill animals, such as insects, that attack crops or livestock.

photochemical smog
A brown haze produced when strong sunlight falls on polluted air. The energy in the sunlight makes pollutants react with each other.

photosynthesis
A process that plants, algae, and some bacteria use to grow. During photosynthesis they collect energy from sunlight and use it to make complex chemicals from carbon dioxide and water.

sustainable
A word used to describe an activity that continues indefinitely without running out of the things that it needs to work.

vertebrate
An animal that has a backbone. Vertebrates include fish, amphibians, reptiles, birds, and mammals.

Fossilized skull of *Tyrannosaurus rex*

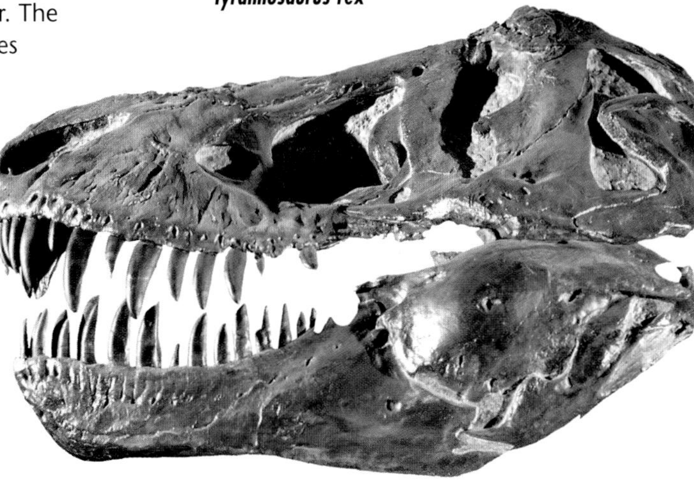

Index

Acknowledgments

The publisher would like to thank the following for permission to reproduce their material. Every care has been taken to trace copyright holders. However, if there have been unintentional omissions or failure to trace copyright holders, we apologize and will, if informed, endeavor to make corrections in any future edition.

Key: *b* = bottom, *c* = center, *l* = left, *r* = right, *t* = top

Cover*l* Lonely Planet Images; cover *c* Nature History Picture Agency; cover *r* Corbis; 1 Still Pictures (Still); 2–3 Edifice; 4–5 Still; 7 Corbis; 8–9 Getty Stone; 8*tr* Getty Imagebank; 9*tr* Science Photo Library (SPL); 10–11 Lonely Planet; 10*bl* Still; 11*cl* SPL; 11*br* Nature Picture Library (Naturepl); 12 SPL; 13 Sue Cunningham; 14 Lonely Planet; 15*br* Lonely Planet; 16*tl* Corbis; 16*bl* Still; 16*bc* Still; 17 Getty Stone; 18 Lonely Planet; 19 Still; 20–21 Corbis; 20 Corbis; 21*t* Corbis; 22–23 Corbis; 22*bl* Still; 23*tr* Corbis; 24*br* Corbis; 24–25 Corbis; 25*tc* Lonely Planet; 25*tr* Lonely Planet; 26–27 Corbis; 26*cl* Corbis; 26–27*t* Corbis; 27*tr* Corbis; 28–29 Getty Taxi; 28–29*t* Corbis; 30–31 Corbis; 30*tl* Corbis; 31*tl* Corbis; 31*br* Still; 32*bl* Still; 32–33*t* Still; 33*tr* Lonely Planet; 33*b* Still; 34–35 Getty Imagebank; 34 Corbis; 35*tr* Still; 36–37 Alamy; 36*bl* SPL; 38*tl* Corbis; 38*bl* SPL; 39*tl* Alamy; 39*tr* SPL; 39*br* Corbis; 40–41 Getty Imagebank; 41*cl* Lonely Planet; 41*br* Zefa; 42–43*t* Lonely Planet; 42*cl* Ardea; 42*b* Getty Taxi; 43*br* Alamy; 44 Corbis; 45 Ecoscene; 46 Art Archive; 47*br* Greenpeace; 48–49*t* Sandia National Laboratories; 48*bl* SPL; 49*cl* Getty Stone; 49*br* Lonely Planet; 50–51 Corbis; 50*bl* SPL; 50–51*t* Corbis; 51*tr* Still; 51*br* SPL; 52–53 Alamy; 53*tl* Alamy; 53*tr* Alamy; 53*b* Zefa; 54*tl* Corbis; 54*bl* Oxford Scientific Films; 54–55*b* Getty Imagebank; 55*tr* Corbis; 58 SPL; 59 Corbis; 60*bl* Corbis; 61*t* National Geographic Society; 61*b* SPL; 64 Still

The publisher would like to thank the following illustrators:
Steve Weston (Linden Artists); Encompass Graphics